Pursuing the Heart of God

BOOK *2*

Another 30-Day Journey to Deeper Intimacy with God

SINDY NAGEL

Copyright © 2021 Sindy Nagel

All Rights Reserved

The NIV Bible does not capitalize the God pronouns. However, the author capitalized all God pronouns (i.e. He, His, Him, Himself, Me, My, Mine, Our, Ours, You, Yours, etc.) in all Bible verses and quotes listed in this book in order to give our awesome God the honor and glory He deserves.

ISBN: 978-0-9969934-4-9 (Paperback)
ISBN: 978-0-9969934-5-6 (Kindle)
ISBN: 978-1-7368521-1-8 (Audio Book)

Edited by Monique Bos

Cover design by Angie (Pro_ebookcovers) at www.fiverr.com
Cover photo and design by Michelle Wise at www.wisephotography.com

Printed in the United States of America.

*A huge "**Thank You**" to my husband, Doug Nagel, who is my biggest supporter and encourager; to my friend, Kellie Cody, for his review and recommendations; and to my editor, Monique Bos, for her help not only in editing, but also in helping me clarify some of the intended messages.*

A message received directly from the mouth of God needs to be treasured and well-handled. To read God's Word and hear the voice of God within you is to experience a full life. To hear God's voice is one thing, but to listen and obey is the most excellent way.—Sindy Nagel

Table of Contents

Pursuing the Heart of God - Book 2 - The Journey

** BEGINNING OF SIX BONUS DAYS **

Pursuing the Heart of God - Refresher

I am so excited that you purchased this **Book 2** in the **Pursuing the Heart of God Series** and decided to continue with another guided 30-day journey in your pursuit of becoming 'a person after God's own heart'. In case a little time passed between your reading of the first book and this Book 2, I have included here a short review and refresher of what we covered in the first three chapters of Book 1.

Refresher: Book 1, Chapter One – First Things First

In order to know the heart of God and hear His voice within, you must first accept the fact that Jesus Christ is the only way to God the Father. You must believe, in faith, that Jesus Christ, the Son of God, came in to the world in the flesh, to be the sacrificial Lamb of God to die in your place, saving you from your sin, and believe God raised Him from the dead. Jesus is alive!

When you say a prayer of invitation, inviting Jesus into your heart to be your Savior and the Lord of your life, God puts His Holy Spirit in your heart as a deposit guaranteeing what is to come (see 2 Corinthians 1:22). When you believe in Jesus Christ, you are marked in Him with a seal, the promised Holy Spirit (see Ephesians 1:13). You become a child of God. You can experience the full life Jesus Christ came to give you here on earth, and you will spend eternal life in relationship with God.

As a Christ follower, since the Holy Spirit lives in your heart, you can expect and believe that you have the ability to hear and recognize His voice in your thoughts. John 8:47 says, "Whoever belongs to God hears what God says…" In order to hear God's voice, it helps to gain a better understanding of Who the person of the Holy Spirit is and all that He does for us.

To more fully know and appreciate the Holy Spirit, I suggest you do a treasure hunt, or a word search, in your Bible concordance.

Look up the words **'Holy'** and **'Spirit'**. You may not find the two words listed together as headings in your concordance. However, take time to read through and meditate on all the verse references that list the words 'Holy Spirit' together under the word 'Holy' in your concordance. Also review all the verses listed under the word 'Spirit' where the word is capitalized. Look up all these verses and study the surrounding passages to gain a better understanding of the Holy Spirit's role in your life. This study of the Scripture may help convince you that in order to fulfill His role, the Holy Spirit does to speak to you. Your role is to regularly tune in to His voice and listen.

If you still do not experience success in hearing and recognizing the voice of God within, it might be a good idea to remove any roadblocks that stand in the way of your communication with God. Ask the Holy Spirit to convict you of anything you may need to change in your life in order to knock down these barriers. Here are a few ideas to consider; do any of these seven things create a roadblock for you in hearing God's voice: doubt, fear, pride, worry, busyness, sin, or an unwillingness to forgive? Examine your heart closely, and do what it takes to clear your path to experiencing two-way conversation with God.

Refresher: Book 1, Chapter Two – Knowing God and Discerning His Voice

Our relationship with God is similar to our other relationships in that, in order to know someone intimately, we need to accumulate hours and hours of conversations with them, getting to know them inside and out. The Bible is referred to as God's love letter to His children. To know God better and discern His voice, we must spend time reading His love letter to us—His Word. In reading His Word in Scripture, we will see an accurate, truthful picture of Who God is, His character, and His heart for His children—for you. We can also gain a better understanding of the Trinity—three Persons, yet one God: Father, Son, and Holy Spirit.

It's also essential that we comprehend that our enemy, the devil, also interjects his thoughts into ours. So in order to discern the voice of God from the voice of Satan in our thoughts, we must also know the character and the ways of the devil. Again, a word search of the words 'devil', 'enemy', 'evil', and 'Satan' in your Bible concordance will begin to provide you Scriptural truth to read and digest about this enemy, the devil. Also refer back to the tables labeled, **Discern What You Hear**[1] and **Discern Who You Hear**[2] shown in Book 1, Chapter Two.

Here's another idea we discussed:

> There are at least seven ways we hear from God, including but not limited to 1) the rare occurrence of an audible voice, 2) the more commonly occurring inaudible voice in our thoughts, 3) the Holy Spirit's illumination of Scripture, 4) dreams and visions, 5) divine revelation, 6) divinely directed desire, or 7) the words of another individual.

> In this book we will focus on only two: 1) hearing God's voice through His written Word (*logos* in Greek), which is for all humanity, and 2) hearing God's voice through His spoken word (*rhēma* in Greek). *Rhēma* is the means by which God chooses to communicate His heart, His will, and His wisdom to an individual, specifically for that person's life, situation, or circumstance.[3]

---

[1] Sindy Nagel, *Pursuing the Heart of God: A 30-day Journey to Deeper Intimacy with God* (self-pub., Amazon KDP: 2021), 30.
[2] Nagel, *Pursuing the Heart of God*, 31.
[3] Nagel, *Pursuing the Heart of God*, 32.

When you first begin listening for God's voice within, you may hear only a word or two, and as you become more seasoned in recognizing God's voice, you may hear phrases, sentences, and more. Good things come in small packages. Whatever whispers you hear God speak, small or large, should be confirmed in His written Word and recorded in a journal.

Again, use the concordance in your Bible to look up the word(s) you hear God speak. As you scan through the list of references for the word(s) you heard, pay attention to the prompting of the Holy Spirit Who will illumine or highlight a verse or two for you. Then, turn to the verse(s) in Scripture and read the verse(s) and surrounding passage.

Watch for confirmation in Scripture of what you heard Him say. Also be ready for God to use His written Word to expand on whatever He whispered to you in your thoughts. It's like discovering a buried treasure, time and again. It will leave you hungering for more opportunities to hear from God. Make time for listening to God whenever possible. You'll be really glad you did!

Refresher: Book 1, Chapter Three – Becoming a Person After God's Own Heart

David is an example of a person who God Himself termed, "a man after My own heart; he will do everything I want him to do" (see Acts 13:22). When we examine David's life, it seems the characteristics that earned him that accolade were: humility, obedience to God's instructions and commands, a passion for knowing God's heart and desires, moving into God's power and purposes in his life, and pursuing God even in weakness.

Another Biblical example of a person who pursued and pleased the Lord's heart is found in the story of the two sisters of Lazarus,

Martha and Mary of Bethany. We see that Jesus was most delighted with Mary's choice to sit at His feet and listen to what He said (see Luke 10:38-42). Whenever we make time to meet with God and listen to His voice, He is pleased.

God desires to be in close relationship with you, His child, through daily two-way conversation. He wants you to put Him first making time to sit at His feet and listen to every word that falls from His mouth. He loves you and pursues you passionately, and He desires that you also pursue Him enthusiastically. In Jeremiah 29:13, God says, "You will seek Me and find Me when you seek Me with all your heart." Once you find Him, be sure to write down everything you hear from Him. Discover Who He is and how He feels about you. Then live in the power and purpose of the life He designed you for. Jesus came to give you life in the fullest. Hearing God's voice within you will fill you to overflowing!

Introduction to the Next 30-Day Journey

The next 30 days of inspirations encompass another guided tour of the journey to deeper intimacy with God. I presume you have completed the first 30-day journey in *Pursuing the Heart of God (Book 1)*. Therefore, this is the next 30 days of encouraging messages from God and a guide to spending time alone with the Lord. This journey resumes the reader in the daily practice of putting God first, meeting with Him away from noise and distractions to better hear God's voice and more genuinely know His heart.

The daily inspirations included in this 30-day journey were written with the assumption that you have already accepted Jesus Christ as your Savior and invited Him into your heart to be the Lord of your life. When you do so, God seals you as His child for all eternity and sends His Holy Spirit to dwell in your heart. The Holy Spirit is the voice of God within you! Hearing the voice of God within you and living in step with the Holy Spirit are two keys to experiencing the full, abundant life Jesus came to give us.

In these daily readings, you will begin to rely on the Holy Spirit as He convicts you of your sin, teaches you the Lord's ways, reveals the heart of God, helps you know God's will, instructs you in the understanding of God's Word, inspires you to be obedient to God's commands, and allows you to experience all of God's best blessings for you in a Spirit-led, Spirit-filled, abundant life.

My prayer for you is that, throughout this next 30-day journey, you may continue to: 1) learn to discern the voice of God within you, 2) realize a greater intimacy with the Lord as you discover deeper places of His heart, and 3) experience the full life God intended for you from the beginning. This journey requires that you daily set aside time to be alone with God and dive in with all your heart in order to pursue and know His. Run for the prize and cherish God's heart for you, as He gives you the desires of yours!

To best prepare for your daily meeting time with the Lord, find a location where you can consistently meet alone with God each day to work through these inspirations. It may be a room in your home, a special place in nature, a favorite spot you drive to, or a quiet nook in your workplace. Next, pick a time of day that works best for you. You will probably need at least 30 minutes to read and answer the questions each day—maybe more time if you have it. If you're an early bird, set the alarm 30 minutes earlier to get up and meet with the Lord. If you find yourself most alert at noon, meet with the Lord during lunch. Or if you're a night owl, make sure you spend time with God later in the evening.

Another key to preparing to meet with the Lord is to find a location away from people and noise, where you will not be interrupted, as well as a time of day when you are most awake and alert. The more consistent you can be with your place and time, the more apt you will be to make this God meeting work for you. Warning: As you sit alone in the serenity, you may have a tendency to fall asleep. This is wonderful—it means you are at peace with God. However, do whatever you need to do to keep yourself awake.

Every day in this 30-day journey is formatted the same. You will begin your conversation with the Lord in the **Ask God** section, where you will ask Him some questions on different topics to reflect on. You may choose to read silently to the Lord or ask Him aloud. Imagine Jesus sitting with you in your quiet place and speaking with you in two-way conversation as a friend. Ask Him questions, and then wait for His reply. Write whatever you hear!

The sections titled **Listen to God - A Message from His Heart** are messages God gave me for me and you, His children. God shares His heart with answers to the questions interwoven with His words and phrases from Scripture shown *italicized*, words of encouragement, instructions, warnings, and more. As you read through this section, watch for words or phrases that stand out to you, warm your heart, or speak directly to a situation you currently experience. Chances are good this is the Holy Spirit speaking to your heart from the words written in these sections. Be ready to explore in greater depth these special words and phrases highlighted or illuminated by the Holy Spirit when you complete the questions in the **Personal Reflections** section.

The sections titled **Supporting Scripture** are the full quoted verses that are paraphrased in the **Listen to God** section above it. Notice how God's written Word is interwoven into His spoken word in the **Listen to God** section. Many times when God speaks to you, you will hear Scripture intermingled.

The **Personal Reflections** section will guide you through a time of meeting with the Lord, reflecting on the **Listen to God** section, asking Him additional questions, and listening for His whispers in your thoughts. Be sure to write every word or thought you have during this time of reflection and connection with the Lord. Do not discount any word or thought. Do not assume all these words and thoughts are your own. Some may originate from God. Remember, as you begin to recognize God's voice, you may hear only a word or two. As you practice listening to God, you may begin to hear His words to you in phrases, then sentences and more.

The **Identify the Voice** section will help you discern the voice of God from the voice of Satan in your thoughts recorded in the **Personal Reflections** section. Any remaining thoughts are your own. Be sure to refer back to Chapter Two of *Pursuing the Heart of God – Book 1* for more clarification on discerning God's character and thoughts from the enemy's. If you find that you regularly identify Satan's voice in your thoughts, make a little time every day to pray, clothing yourself in the Armor of God (see Ephesians 6:10-18) and standing firm against the attacks of the enemy. Ask God to bind up the enemy and all evil in the name of Jesus Christ, by His blood shed on the cross. Verbally, aloud, rebuke Satan, and do not make any vows or agreements with him. Claim the victory of Jesus' death and resurrection, and walk in the authority and freedom He gives us.

The **Going Deeper** section will guide the Christ follower who is more seasoned in listening to God's voice into an additional time of in-depth, two-way conversation with all three Persons of the Trinity. It also provides additional practice for the new listener to God's voice who has more time to spend in conversation with God each day. You may continue your time with God during your current meeting, or you may choose to complete the **Personal Reflections** section in the morning, and then meet with God at the end of the day to complete the **Going Deeper** section.

The **Prayer** sections will help guide your 'talking to God' time. Feel free to add on your own praises and petitions.

It's a great idea to keep a separate journal or notebook where you may record additional prayers, inspirations, and thoughts that do not fit in the blank spaces provided in this book. Be sure to date your journal, including the Day #__ and daily title from this book, when you record your thoughts and conversations with God. It's fun to return to these journal entries to remember the truth revealed by the Holy Spirit in your thoughts and to see your growth in hearing and discerning the voice of God within you.

I encourage you to passionately pursue God's heart all hours of the day, every day. It will be well worth the time and effort! Have fun on this next 30-day adventure with God!

Pursuing the Heart of God - Book 2

Day 1 ♥♥ Child of God

Ask God:

Lord, what does it mean that I am Your child? How have I earned that awesome title? To what do I owe the amazing privilege of being a child of God?

Listen to God - A Message from His Heart:

My child, you have not earned this privilege of being called a child of God. It was given to you when you were created by Me and when you were reborn again by faith in My Son, Jesus Christ. *I knit you together in your mother's womb.* I created you because I love you. *I know you by name, and you have found favor with Me.*

Before you were born, I set you apart and called you by name. I have lavished My great love on you; you are My child. I desire a more cherished relationship with you on a daily basis. You are My blessed child, and I love to spend time with you alone. Will you put Me first and make Me your highest priority?

In Christ Jesus, you are My child through faith. Your sin separated you from Me. However, I provided the way to reconciliation with Me. When you received Christ as your Savior and believed in the risen Jesus Christ as My Son, *I gave you the right to become My child,* adopted by Me, through faith in Christ.

For My Son, Jesus Christ, has said, *"Truly I tell you, unless you change and become like little children, you will never enter the kingdom of heaven. Therefore, whoever takes the lowly position of this child is the greatest in the kingdom of heaven. And whoever welcomes one such child in My name welcomes Me."* Take on the nature of a child of God, a lowly infant who is dependent, pure, humble, meek, inquisitive, unassuming, obedient, passionate, loving, forgiving, and merciful.

You are a child of God, and therefore you are led by the Spirit of God. The Spirit you received when you confessed Jesus as your Savior and Lord *brought about your adoption. And by Him you are given the right to cry, "Abba, Father." The Spirit Himself testifies with your spirit that you are God's child. Now if you are His child, then you are His heir—heir of God and co-heir with Christ, if indeed you share in His sufferings in order that you may also share in His glory.*

You are human, and you disobey Me occasionally. *However, because you are My child, whom I love, I discipline you when you need it, in order that you may share in My holiness. No discipline seems pleasant at the time, but painful. Later on, however, it produces a harvest of righteousness and peace for those who have been trained by it.* Consider yourself a legitimate child of God when I love you enough to discipline you in the training of the Lord for a future harvest of righteousness and peace.

My blessed one, being a child of God is a privilege. It is an honor and a freedom. Along with any hardships you endure, as My child you will also experience My favor in life. I will take care of you and provide for you. I will protect you and shield you. I will rescue you and uphold you. I am your loving Father, the great Shepherd of His sheep. You are My little lamb that I love dearly.

Psalm 139:13; Exodus 33:12; Jeremiah 1:5;
1 John 3:1; Galatians 3:26; John 1:12;
Matthew 18:2-4; Romans 8:14-17; Hebrews 12:7-11

Supporting Scripture:

For You created my inmost being; You knit me together in my mother's womb.—Psalm 139:13

"You have said, 'I know you by name and you have found favor with Me.'"—Exodus 33:12

"Before I formed you in the womb I knew you, before you were born I set you apart…"—Jeremiah 1:5

See what great love the Father has lavished on us, that we should be called children of God! And that is what we are! The reason the world did not know us is that it did not know Him.—1 John 3:1

So in Christ Jesus you are all children of God through faith.—Galatians 3:26

Yet to all who did receive Him, to those who believed in His name, He gave the right to become children of God.—John 1:12

[2]He called a little child to Him, and placed the child among them. [3]And He said: "Truly I tell you, unless you change and become like little children, you will never enter the kingdom of heaven. [4]Therefore, whoever takes the lowly position of this child is the greatest in the kingdom of heaven."—Matthew 18:2-4

[14]For those who are led by the Spirit of God are children of God. [15]The Spirit you received does not make you slaves, so that you live in fear again; rather, the Spirit you received brought about your adoption to sonship. And by Him we cry, "*Abba*, Father." [16]The Spirit Himself testifies with our spirit that we are God's children. [17]Now if we are children, then we are heirs—heirs of God and co-heirs with Christ, if indeed we share in His sufferings in order that we may also share in His glory.—Romans 8:14-17

[7]Endure hardship as discipline; God is treating you as His children. For what children are not disciplined by their father? [8]If you are not disciplined—and everyone undergoes discipline—then you are not legitimate, not true sons and daughters at all. [9]Moreoever, we have all had human fathers who disciplined us and we respected them for it. How much more should we submit to the Father of spirits

and live! [10]They disciplined us for a little while as they thought best; but God disciplines us for our good, in order that we may share in His holiness. [11]No discipline seems pleasant at the time, but painful. Later on, however, it produces a harvest of righteousness and peace for those who have been trained by it.— Hebrews 12:7-11

Prayer:

Father in heaven, thank You so much for creating me, loving me, and adopting me as Your child. I am so blessed to be included as Your little lamb in Your sheepfold. Thank You for Your favor as a child of the King. Thank You for Your protection and provision. I live to bring You all the glory, honor, and praise You are due. Holy Spirit, please share more of Your passions with me right now as we sit in conversation with one another. In Jesus' name I pray. Amen.

Personal Reflections:

1) From the **Listen to God** section above, pick out a phrase or two that spoke directly to your heart today. Write the words here:

2) As you re-read and think about the words you wrote above, record any additional words or thoughts that come to your mind:

3) Which of the words or thoughts you recorded above might be from God? Underline or highlight them. Does any Scripture come to mind as you re-read what you've written above? If so, write the portion of Scripture that you recall:

4) Turn to the concordance of your Bible and look up one of the words you recalled from Scripture. Scan the verses cited under the word you have referenced in the concordance and record the references of one or two of the verses that the Holy Spirit illumines with special meaning for you today:

5) Turn to each of the references you recorded above. Read the verse and the surrounding passages. Do any additional words or phrases have special meaning for you today? Perhaps something you needed to hear? Wisdom for a problem you face? An answer to a question? A timely word for a difficult circumstance you currently navigate? If so, record the Scripture or words here:

6) What further question(s) do you have for God today? Write them here:

7) Seek God for answers to the question(s) you wrote above. Ask God one of the questions, and then, sit quietly and wait for His reply. Record the first thought that enters your mind. Write all the thoughts you have as you sit and listen to the Lord:

8) Chances are good that the thoughts you recorded as you sat quietly waiting for the Lord's response were indeed thoughts whispered to you by the Holy Spirit within you. Re-read the thoughts above and ask God to confirm the thoughts that are from Him. Record any new inspirations you hear in your thoughts now:

Identify the Voice:

Re-read the responses you've written to the previous few questions. Run them through the tests below. In each test, the characteristic of God's voice is listed before the OR and the characteristic of Satan's voice is listed after it. Do those thoughts recorded in the section above:

    a.   Align with the character of God OR the ways of Satan?
    b.   Agree with the Word of God OR contradict it?
    c.   Produce the peace of God in your soul OR stir up strife?
    d.   Convict you OR condemn you?
    e.   Bring spiritual clarity OR confusion?
    f.   Offer the Lord's wisdom, instruction, comfort, and encouragement OR cause you to feel doubt, fear, worry, or shame?
    g.   Bring emotional healing OR cause additional emotional pain?

Using the above tests as your guide, draw a line through any thoughts in the previous section that might be from your enemy, the devil. Take a minute to rebuke Satan aloud. Do not believe his lies or buy in to his accusations or condemnations that you identify in your thoughts.

Going Deeper in Two-way Conversation with God:

    1)   Father God, will You now speak to me personally about my privilege and role as Your child? What do You desire from me? (Record all the words and thoughts He gives you now.)

2) Jesus, my Savior and Lord, thank You for providing the way back to God, the Father. Thank You for the many blessings my faith in You affords me. Please tell me what my faith in You offers me as God's heir, co-heir with You. (Write whatever pops into your mind right now as you listen to His voice.)

3) Holy Spirit, help me assume the lowly position as Your little child. May I desire to be led by You in everything I do and say. Teach me how to remain in step with You all throughout my day. (Journal all ideas you hear in your thoughts.)

Review the thoughts God gave you above. Is there a common theme in the impressions you recorded? Perhaps you heard a word that especially warms your heart today? What Scripture comes to mind as you review your notes? Use the concordance of your Bible to look up a word that especially stood out to you or a word that you heard more than once in your thoughts. Scan the list of occurrences of that word cited in Scripture. When you see a verse in the concordance that has special meaning for you today, the

Holy Spirit is highlighting that verse for you. Turn to that passage of Scripture and read it. Write the verse here. Then, write all further insights and confirmations the Holy Spirit gives you as you read and ponder God's Word for you today.

Prayer:

Father, Son, and Holy Spirit, thank You for Your love and the ability to hear Your voice in my thoughts. Thank You all for the work You have done in my life to bring me into a saving relationship with the Lord, an abundant life on this earth, and an eternity in heaven with You. I am truly blessed to be called a child of God, and I am eternally grateful for this privilege. Spirit, please lead me and guide me through this life, so that I may let my light shine for others to see Your goodness and Your grace, bringing all the glory to My Father in heaven. In the name of Jesus I pray. Amen.

Pursuing the Heart of God - Book 2

Day 2 ♥♥ Pray Continually

Ask God:

Lord, what does it mean to pray continually? Do I need to breathe a prayer all day long to You? How do I work this into my busy life? What do You require of me and desire from me with regard to prayer?

Listen to God - A Message from His Heart:

My darling child, continual conversational prayer is the main way I communicate with you through the Holy Spirit dwelling in you. I desire that you live your life, busy as it is, in an attitude of prayer, talking to Me and listening to Me throughout your day, all day, every day. That means that as you go about your daily activities, make decisions, and plan for your future, you seek Me in prayer. As you practice this more, eventually it will become your first instinct to speak with Me in every situation, not only in trials and challenges.

Consult with Me to gain the wisdom you need to make all your decisions, large and small. *Ask Me for anything*, grandiose or minuscule, *and it will be yours when you believe you will have what you ask for*. I want to be involved in every area of your life. I want you to depend on Me for your wisdom, your direction, and your strength.

Do not be anxious about anything, but in every situation, by prayer and petition, with thanksgiving, present your requests to Me, and My peace, which transcends all understanding, will guard your heart and your mind in Christ Jesus. I will calm your fears and give you the courage for every battle, the wisdom for every circumstance, the strength for every challenge.

You may *rejoice always*, because of the confidence you have in knowing that I am God, I am in control, and I will provide for you in all situations. You may be free to *give thanks in all circumstances* for the same reason. Prayers of gratitude and thanksgiving shall become a daily devotion for you as well. Tune in to the Spirit of God within you. Remain *in step with the Spirit. The fruit of the Spirit is joy*. Let others see My joy in you, even in the middle of the storms. Joy comes from the confidence you receive when you place your trust in Me through prayer.

It is possible that you can go about your daily routine maintaining an ongoing conversation with Me. Pay attention to the voice of My Holy Spirit inside you. He will direct your thoughts and stimulate your memory, reminding you to seek Me and speak to Me often. You simply need to be more mindful of My continual presence through the Spirit within you. I am with you at all times. I hope to hear from you in all circumstances. I desire that you depend on Me for everything. *Ask Me for anything in My name, and I will do it.*

Pray to Me about anything and everything. I *hear all your cries*, and I answer every one in My perfect way and timing. I am here and ready to answer your pleas for recollection and wisdom, whether you're locating a lost set of keys or making the decision to buy a new home. I am for you, not against you. I favor you; I do not disregard you. I am at your side, on your side in all situations. I love you, My child. Will you love Me with all your heart by seeking Me first, before you make your plans and decisions?

When you pray frequently, you sustain the intimate fellowship I desire. You will learn to trust Me more when you continually work on developing a more cherished connection with Me daily. You will see that I am *compassionate, gracious, slow to anger, abounding in love and faithfulness.* You will acknowledge I am your Lord, your Warrior, your Confidante, and your Friend. I am your loving Father, and I desire to hear from you and speak to you more regularly throughout your day. I do not forget you; please do not forget Me. I love you, My friend.

James 1:5-6; Philippians 4:6-7; 1 Thessalonians 5:16-18;
Galatians 5:22-23; John 14:13-14; Psalm 6:9; Exodus 34:6-7

Supporting Scripture:

[5]If any of you lacks wisdom, you should ask God, Who gives generously to all without finding fault, and it will be given to you. [6]But when you ask, you must believe and not doubt, because the one who doubts is like a wave of the sea, blown and tossed by the wind.—James 1:5-6

[6]Do not be anxious about anything, but in every situation, by prayer and petition, with thanksgiving, present your requests to God. [7]And the peace of God, which transcends all understanding, will guard your hearts and your minds in Christ Jesus.—Philippians 4:6-7

[16]Rejoice always, [17]pray continually, [18]give thanks in all circumstances; for this is God's will for you in Christ Jesus.—1 Thessalonians 5:16-18

[22]But the fruit of the Spirit is love, joy, peace, forbearance, kindness, goodness, faithfulness, [23]gentleness, and self-control. Against such things there is no law.—Galatians 5:22-23

[13]"And I will do whatever you ask in My name, so that the Father may be glorified in the Son. [14]You may ask Me for anything in My name, and I will do it."—John 14:13-14

The LORD has heard my cry for mercy; the LORD accepts my prayer.—Psalm 6:9

[6]And He passed in front of Moses, proclaiming "The LORD, the LORD, the compassionate and gracious God, slow to anger, abounding in love and faithfulness, [7]maintaining love to thousands, and forgiving wickedness, rebellion and sin..."—Exodus 34:6-7

Prayer:

Dear Lord, I give thanks that You are available to speak with me all hours of the day and night. Please help me develop the practice of speaking with You more frequently throughout my day. I want to be dependent on You and honor You by putting You first in my life. I also desire a deeper connection and a more intimate relationship with You. That comes only by communicating with you more regularly. Holy Spirit, please speak to me specifically right now about how I can accomplish this goal. Please give me ideas that I can work on with You. In Jesus' name, I pray. Amen.

Personal Reflections:

1) From the **Listen to God** section above, pick out a phrase or two that spoke directly to your heart today. Write the words here:

2) As you re-read and think about the words you wrote above, record any additional words or thoughts that come to your mind:

3) Which of the words or thoughts you recorded above might be from God? Underline or highlight them. Does any Scripture come to mind as you re-read what you've written above? If so, write the portion of Scripture that you recall:

4) Turn to the concordance of your Bible and look up one of the words you recalled from Scripture. Scan the verses cited under the word you have referenced in the concordance and record the references of one or two of the verses that the Holy Spirit illumines with special meaning for you today:

5) Turn to each of the references you recorded above. Read the verse and the surrounding passages. Do any additional words or phrases have special meaning for you today? Perhaps something you needed to hear? Wisdom for a problem you face? An answer to a question? A timely word for a difficult circumstance you currently navigate? If so, record the Scripture or words here:

6) What further question(s) do you have for God today? Write them here:

7) Seek God for answers to the question(s) you wrote above. Ask God one of the questions, and then, sit quietly and wait for His reply. Record the first thought that enters your mind. Write all the thoughts you have as you sit and listen to the Lord:

8) Chances are good that the thoughts you recorded as you sat quietly waiting for the Lord's response were indeed thoughts whispered to you by the Holy Spirit within you. Re-read the thoughts above and ask God to confirm the thoughts that are from Him. Record any new inspirations you hear in your thoughts now:

Identify the Voice:

Re-read the responses you've written to the previous few questions. Run them through the tests below. In each test, the characteristic of God's voice is listed before the OR and the characteristic of

Satan's voice is listed after it. Do those thoughts recorded in the section above:

a. Align with the character of God OR the ways of Satan?
b. Agree with the Word of God OR contradict it?
c. Produce the peace of God in your soul OR stir up strife?
d. Convict you OR condemn you?
e. Bring spiritual clarity OR confusion?
f. Offer the Lord's wisdom, instruction, comfort, and encouragement OR cause you to feel doubt, fear, worry, or shame?
g. Bring emotional healing OR cause additional emotional pain?

Using the above tests as your guide, draw a line through any thoughts in the previous section that might be from your enemy, the devil. Take a minute to rebuke Satan aloud. Do not believe his lies or buy in to his accusations or condemnations that you identify in your thoughts.

Going Deeper in Two-way Conversation with God:

1) Father in heaven, please speak to me personally about how I might implement this 'pray continually' attitude. (Record all ideas and thoughts He gives you.)

2) Jesus, share with me how You maintain an attitude of praying continually. How do I accomplish this in my busy life? What do You require of me? (Write the impressions and thoughts you receive.)

3) Holy Spirit, please spark my memory, reminding me all day long to think about communicating with God as I carry out every activity. Help me discern Your voice and Your leading in this area. Please show me how You work in my heart to help me carry out this request. (Journal all you hear in your thoughts right now.)

Review the thoughts God gave you above. Is there a common theme in the impressions you recorded? Perhaps you heard a word that especially warms your heart today? What Scripture comes to mind as you review your notes? Use the concordance of your Bible to look up a word that especially stood out to you or a word that you heard more than once in your thoughts. Scan the list of occurrences of that word cited in Scripture. When you see a verse in the concordance that has special meaning for you today, the

Holy Spirit is highlighting that verse for you. Turn to that passage of Scripture and read it. Write the verse here. Then, write all further insights and confirmations the Holy Spirit gives you as you read and ponder God's Word for you today.

Prayer:

Most High God, thank You that I may approach You with the confidence of knowing that I am Your child and You hear every word I speak. Lord, please help me discern Your voice within and hear every word You speak to me. Lord, I am so grateful that I can experience a close relationship with You. Help me to maintain this two-way conversation with You that is so life changing and exhilarating. To me, hearing Your voice equals the abundant life Jesus came to give me. Thank You that prayer is one of the ways I can experience intimacy with you. In Jesus' name I pray. Amen.

Pursuing the Heart of God - Book 2

Day 3 ♥♥ Blessed to Be a Blessing

Ask God:

Lord, I am so grateful for all that You have blessed me with. How may I be a blessing to others? How might I pay it forward for Your sake? What is Your plan and purpose for my life? How might I best serve You, bring glory to Your name, and bless Your children in the process?

Listen to God - A Message from His Heart:

My child, *I have blessed you to be a blessing.* Just as I blessed Abraham to be a blessing, so I have blessed you to be a benefit to others. *I have given you much, and much will be required of you. I have entrusted you with much, so I ask much more of you.* Will you prove faithful? *It is more blessed to give than to receive.* Give generously out of the abundance you have received from Me.

Blessed are you when you revere My name and take delight in My commands. Blessed are the ones who seek Me and find My *wisdom and understanding*, who *listen to Me and find life in My wisdom.*

I do not bless you so that you may keep it to yourself. *Freely you have received*; now freely pass along your blessings to others. In the spirit of giving, be generous with your gifts; give liberally, as you have received generously from Me. This includes the gifts of love and forgiveness.

Do not be stingy in your giving. You have been blessed with much, so you must, in turn, contribute much to the well-being of others. Give food to the poor and spiritual food to the poor in spirit. Share a meal along with the good news of the gospel. *Those who give to the poor will lack nothing.* I consider you *pure and faultless when you look after the widow and the orphan.* This is a cause I feel strongly about.

Do not keep to yourself what you have learned in strife. Be a blessing to others by sharing your experiences and what I have taught you. A teacher does not withhold the blessing of experiential learning. Let others learn from your mistakes whenever they are willing to listen. Share your story, the redemption story I have written in your life, as well as My story of love in the Bible.

Be prepared at all times to give an account for the hope which you have in Christ Jesus. Share the message of the gospel and offer the prayer of invitation when the Holy Spirit prompts you. Do not shrink back from My requests. Whenever possible, guide others into a saving knowledge of Jesus Christ.

Do not store up for yourself treasures on earth, but store up treasures in heaven, where nothing will destroy them. You have been blessed so richly, both in this life and in eternity, because of My mercy and grace. Will you now be a blessing to others?

Genesis 12:2-3; Luke 12:48; Acts 20:35; Psalm 94:12;
Psalm 112:1; Proverbs 3:13; Proverbs 8:34-35; Romans 10:12;
Matthew 10:8; Proverbs 28:27; James 1:27; Matthew 6:19-21

Supporting Scripture:

[2]"I will make you into a great nation, and I will bless you; I will make your name great, and you will be a blessing. [3]I will bless those who bless you, and whoever curses you I will curse; and all peoples on earth will be blessed through you."—Genesis 12:2-3

"…From everyone who has been given much, much will be demanded; and from the one who has been entrusted with much, much more will be asked."—Luke 12:48

"In everything I did, I showed you that by this kind of hard work we must help the weak, remembering the words of the Lord Jesus Himself said: 'It is more blessed to give than to receive.'"—Acts 20:35

Blessed is the one You discipline, LORD, the one You teach from Your law.—Psalm 94:12

Praise the LORD. Blessed are those who fear the LORD, who find great delight in His commands.—Psalm 112:1

Blessed are those who find wisdom, those who gain understanding,—Proverbs 3:13

[34]Blessed are those who listen to Me, watching daily at My doors, waiting at My doorway. [35]For those who find Me find life and receive favor from the LORD.—Proverbs 8:34-35

For there is no difference between Jew and Gentile—the same Lord is Lord of all and richly blesses all who call on Him, for, "Everyone who calls on the name of the Lord will be saved."—Romans 10:12

"...Freely you have received; freely give."—Matthew 10:8

Those who give to the poor will lack nothing, but those who close their eyes to them receive many curses.—Proverbs 28:27

Religion that God our Father accepts as pure and faultless is this: to look after orphans and widows in their distress and to keep oneself from being polluted by the world.—James 1:27

[19]"Do not store up for yourselves treasures on earth, where moths and vermin destroy, and where thieves break in and steal. [20]But store up for yourselves treasures in heaven, where moths and vermin do not destroy, and where thieves do not break in and steal.

²¹For where your treasure is, there your heart will be also."— Matthew 6:19-21

Prayer:

Dear Jesus, I am blessed by You to be a blessing to others. Help me use the gifts given to me by the Spirit to benefit the body of Christ, as well as those who do not yet know You as their Savior. Lord Jesus, help me to not be stingy with the gifts You have given me. Let me give generously to others as You have given generously to me. Lord, I ask You to give the voice of Your Spirit to me generously now as we meet for a few moments alone. Lord, allow me to hear Your wisdom and direction for my life. Thank You for the blessing of Your Holy Spirit living in me. I pray that I will always pay attention to Your voice in my thoughts. In Jesus' name I pray. Amen.

Personal Reflections:

1) From the **Listen to God** section above, pick out a phrase or two that spoke directly to your heart today. Write the words here:

2) As you re-read and think about the words you wrote above, record any additional words or thoughts that come to your mind:

3) Which of the words or thoughts you recorded above might be from God? Underline or highlight them. Does any Scripture come to mind as you re-read what you've written above? If so, write the portion of Scripture that you recall:

4) Turn to the concordance of your Bible and look up one of the words you recalled from Scripture. Scan the verses cited under the word you have referenced in the concordance and record the references of one or two of the verses that the Holy Spirit illumines with special meaning for you today:

5) Turn to each of the references you recorded above. Read the verse and the surrounding passages. Do any additional words or phrases have special meaning for you today? Perhaps something you needed to hear? Wisdom for a problem you face? An answer to a question? A timely word for a difficult circumstance you currently navigate? If so, record the Scripture or words here:

6) What further question(s) do you have for God today? Write them here:

7) Seek God for answers to the question(s) you wrote above. Ask God one of the questions, and then, sit quietly and wait for His reply. Record the first thought that enters your mind. Write all the thoughts you have as you sit and listen to the Lord:

8) Chances are good that the thoughts you recorded as you sat quietly waiting for the Lord's response were indeed thoughts whispered to you by the Holy Spirit within you. Re-read the thoughts above and ask God to confirm the thoughts that are from Him. Record any new inspirations you hear in your thoughts now:

Identify the Voice:

Re-read the responses you've written to the previous few questions. Run them through the tests below. In each test, the characteristic of God's voice is listed before the OR and the characteristic of Satan's voice is listed after it. Do those thoughts recorded in the section above:

a. Align with the character of God OR the ways of Satan?
b. Agree with the Word of God OR contradict it?
c. Produce the peace of God in your soul OR stir up strife?
d. Convict you OR condemn you?
e. Bring spiritual clarity OR confusion?
f. Offer the Lord's wisdom, instruction, comfort, and encouragement OR cause you to feel doubt, fear, worry, or shame?
g. Bring emotional healing OR cause additional emotional pain?

Using the above tests as your guide, draw a line through any thoughts in the previous section that might be from your enemy, the devil. Take a minute to rebuke Satan aloud. Do not believe his lies or buy in to his accusations or condemnations that you identify in your thoughts.

Going Deeper in Two-way Conversation with God:

1) Father God, will You now remind me of the blessings I have received from You and how You want me to use those to bless others? (Record all the thoughts that flood your mind right now.)

2) Jesus, my Savior, will You bring to my mind the face of someone You want me to bless today? Then show me, Lord, the best way to show Your love to them. Let me see them through Your eyes and see the real need and the action that will benefit them most. Then give me the courage to give generously to bring glory and honor to You. (Write down the ideas He gives you.)

3) Holy Spirit, may I always be tuned in to Your promptings and Your whispers as You direct me to be a blessing to others. Help me know the means and the extent You desire me to give. Please show Your will for me today. How may I best use my gifts and resources to bless another? Please be specific. (Journal His words and promptings.)

Review the thoughts God gave you above. Is there a common theme in the impressions you recorded? Perhaps you heard a word that especially warms your heart today? What Scripture comes to mind as you review your notes? Use the concordance of your Bible to look up a word that especially stood out to you or a word that you heard more than once in your thoughts. Scan the list of occurrences of that word cited in Scripture. When you see a verse in the concordance that has special meaning for you today, the Holy Spirit is highlighting that verse for you. Turn to that passage of Scripture and read it. Write the verse here. Then, write all further insights and confirmations the Holy Spirit gives you as you read and ponder God's Word for you today.

Prayer:

Almighty God, thank You for sharing Your heart for Your children and ways I might show Your goodness and love to others. I pray that out of my abundance I will always give with a cheerful heart and a generous spirit. Thank You for the ideas You give me on ways I may show Your love to others while blessing them by meeting a need. Lord Jesus, You were the best example of this. Holy Spirit, continue to transform me into the likeness of Christ. In the name of Jesus Christ, Who gave the ultimate gift with His death on the cross, I ask all these things. Amen.

Pursuing the Heart of God - Book 2

Day 4 ♥♥ Trade Your Anxiety for My Peace

Ask God:

Sovereign Lord, You are in control of all things. I confess and acknowledge this fact, and yet many times I forget it, giving way to worry and anxiety instead. Lord, I admit that You will provide for my every need and want. I place my faith and trust in You alone to do so. I trade in my anxiety for Your perfect peace. I lay down my worries, because You are the all-powerful, Almighty God, the one and only supreme Ruler over everything. You love me and take care of me. How do I maintain a life and mindset free from anxiety and full of Your peace?

Listen to God - A Message from His Heart:

My child, give your cares over to Me. I happily take them on. I am the Sovereign Lord, in control of all things, and I will take care of every need you have. *Do not worry about your life: what you will eat and drink, the clothes you will wear. Isn't life more than food and the body more than clothes?* I know your needs, and I will take care of you. *Seek first My kingdom and My righteousness, and all these things will be given to you as well. Do not worry about tomorrow, for tomorrow will worry about itself. Each day has enough trouble of its own.*

Trade in your anxieties, and allow Me to replace them with My perfect peace. *My peace I give you, not as the world gives. Do not let your heart be troubled and do not be afraid.* Leave your worries and your cares at My feet and do not pick them up again. Turn them over to Me. I am the Sovereign Lord, and *in all things I work for the good of those who love Me, who have been called according to My purpose.* That's you! I do this for you.

Lasting peace comes through a relationship with Me. You are My little lamb. I tenderly care for you as a shepherd cares for his sheep. You have access to My peace at all times by the Spirit I have placed in your heart. *You have the same mighty power, through the Holy Spirit living in you, that I exerted when I raised Jesus Christ from the dead.* Be confident in My power; trust in Me forever and remain in perfect peace. Remain in Me and find the peace your soul desires.

As you trust completely in Me, be an eager witness to My kindness. Profess your faith and trust until you, yourself, believe it more fully. Tell others of My goodness and grace, love and mercy, faithfulness and peace. You have traded in your anxieties to experience more of My peace. This is monumental. Worry adds nothing to your life; it sucks the life right out of you. But now that you have freed up so much time you used to spend in worry, you may spend more time working for Me, carrying out My plan and purpose for you.

When your anxiety is great within you, I will console you and bring you joy. When you place your trust in Me, your cares melt away as the snow on a sunny day. I am the *bright Morning Star.* I am here to light your way. Fix your mind upon Me, thoughtfully ponder on My Word and My presence, and your troubles will seem to diminish. *Do not be anxious about anything, but in every situation, by prayer and petition, with thanksgiving, present your requests to Me. And My peace, which transcends all understanding, will guard your heart and your mind in Christ Jesus.*

Trust Me with all your heart, and lean not on your own understanding; in all your ways submit to Me, and I will make your paths straight. My timing and purposes are perfect. I am true to My promises, and I direct your ways. *Cast all your anxiety upon Me because I care for you.* Trade in your heavy load for a lighter one; *take My yoke upon you* and find *rest for your soul.* Trade in your anxieties for My perfect peace. Make this your daily practice.

Resist the temptation to fret and worry; instead claim the peace I freely offer you.

Matthew 6:25; Matthew 6:33-34; John 14:27; Romans 8:28;
Ephesians 1:19-20; Psalm 94:19; Revelation 22:16;
Philippians 4:6-7; Proverbs 3:5-6; 1 Peter 5:7; Matthew 11:29-30

Supporting Scripture:

"Therefore I tell you, do not worry about your life, what you will eat or drink; or about your body; what you will wear. Is not life more than food, and the body more than clothes?"—Matthew 6:25

[33]"But seek first His kingdom and His righteousness, and all these things will be given to you as well. [34]Therefore do not worry about tomorrow, for tomorrow will worry about itself. Each day has enough trouble of its own."—Matthew 6:33-34

"Peace I leave with you; My peace I give you. I do not give to you as the world gives. Do not let your hearts be troubled and do not be afraid."—John 14:27

And we know that in all things God works for the good of those who love Him, who have been called according to His purpose.—Romans 8:28

[19]and His incomparably great power for us who believe. That power is the same as the mighty strength [20]He exerted when He raised Christ from the dead and seated Him at His right hand in the heavenly realms—Ephesians 1:19-20

When anxiety was great within me, Your consolation brought me joy.—Psalm 94:19

"I, Jesus, have sent My angel to give you this testimony for the churches. I am the Root and the Offspring of David, and the bright Morning Star."—Revelation 22:16

[6]Do not be anxious about anything, but in every situation, by prayer and petition, with thanksgiving, present your requests to God. [7]And the peace of God, which transcends all understanding, will guard your hearts and your minds in Christ Jesus.—Philippians 4:6-7

[5]Trust in the LORD with all your heart and lean not on your own understanding; [6]in all your ways submit to Him, and He will make your paths straight.—Proverbs 3:5-6

Cast all your anxiety on Him because He cares for you.—1 Peter 5:7

[29]"Take My yoke upon you and learn from Me, for I am gentle and humble in heart, and you will find rest for your souls. [30]For My yoke is easy and My burden is light."—Matthew 11:29-30

Prayer:

Heavenly Father, so many times I have witnessed Your work behind the scenes, orchestrating all things for my good. You deserve all the credit, honor, and praise for Your goodness and provision. Worry is the product of not trusting fully in You. Lord, please forgive me of my sin. I confess that I do not trust in You as I should. Lord, please show me Your heart right now and make it real to me that You will hold true to Your promises, that I can trust in You completely, and You will not fail me. Holy Spirit, please help me to hear Your voice and cling to Your promises. In Jesus' name, I pray. Amen.

Personal Reflections:

1) From the **Listen to God** section above, pick out a phrase or two that spoke directly to your heart today. Write the words here:

2) As you re-read and think about the words you wrote above, record any additional words or thoughts that come to your mind:

3) Which of the words or thoughts you recorded above might be from God? Underline or highlight them. Does any Scripture come to mind as you re-read what you've written above? If so, write the portion of Scripture that you recall:

4) Turn to the concordance of your Bible and look up one of the words you recalled from Scripture. Scan the verses cited under the word you have referenced in the concordance and record the references of one or two of the verses that the Holy Spirit illumines with special meaning for you today:

5) Turn to each of the references you recorded above. Read the verse and the surrounding passages. Do any additional words or phrases have special meaning for you today? Perhaps something you needed to hear? Wisdom for a problem you face? An answer to a question? A timely word for a difficult circumstance you currently navigate? If so, record the Scripture or words here:

6) What further question(s) do you have for God today? Write them here:

7) Seek God for answers to the question(s) you wrote above. Ask God one of the questions, and then, sit quietly and wait for His reply. Record the first thought that enters your mind. Write all the thoughts you have as you sit and listen to the Lord:

8) Chances are good that the thoughts you recorded as you sat quietly waiting for the Lord's response were indeed thoughts whispered to you by the Holy Spirit within you. Re-read the thoughts above and ask God to confirm the thoughts that are from Him. Record any new inspirations you hear in your thoughts now:

Identify the Voice:

Re-read the responses you've written to the previous few questions. Run them through the tests below. In each test, the characteristic of God's voice is listed before the OR and the characteristic of

Satan's voice is listed after it. Do those thoughts recorded in the section above:

a. Align with the character of God OR the ways of Satan?
b. Agree with the Word of God OR contradict it?
c. Produce the peace of God in your soul OR stir up strife?
d. Convict you OR condemn you?
e. Bring spiritual clarity OR confusion?
f. Offer the Lord's wisdom, instruction, comfort, and encouragement OR cause you to feel doubt, fear, worry, or shame?
g. Bring emotional healing OR cause additional emotional pain?

Using the above tests as your guide, draw a line through any thoughts in the previous section that might be from your enemy, the devil. Take a minute to rebuke Satan aloud. Do not believe his lies or buy in to his accusations or condemnations that you identify in your thoughts.

Going Deeper in Two-way Conversation with God:

1) Abba Father, even though I know in my mind that I can experience Your peace, I still resort to worry and anxiety when I feel out of control. Lord, please calm my fears and teach me how to trust completely in You, the Sovereign God Who is in control of all things. Share Your heart with me now. (Write down the thoughts He gives you.)

2) Prince of Peace, I am so blessed to have You in my life. Thank You for Your peace unlike the world's, the confidence I have by trusting in You completely. Please tell me more about Your peace that transcends understanding. (Record the words and thoughts you receive from Him.)

3) Holy Spirit of God, You are the peace in my heart. Help me remember I have access to Your peace at all times. How may I tap into that lasting peace You so generously provide? (Journal the thoughts He gives you.)

Review the thoughts God gave you above. Is there a common theme in the impressions you recorded? Perhaps you heard a word that especially warms your heart today? What Scripture comes to mind as you review your notes? Use the concordance of your Bible to look up a word that especially stood out to you or a word that you heard more than once in your thoughts. Scan the list of occurrences of that word cited in Scripture. When you see a verse in the concordance that has special meaning for you today, the Holy Spirit is highlighting that verse for you. Turn to that passage of Scripture and read it. Write the verse here. Then, write all further insights and confirmations the Holy Spirit gives you as you read and ponder God's Word for you today.

Prayer:

Most High God, when I think about it more, it is a relief that I am really not in control of anything, because You are in control of everything. There is a freedom in not being responsible for the outcome of any given situation. You created the heavens and the earth. The wind and waves take their commands from You. I am at peace when I trust in You. Lord, remind me often of Your faithfulness and marvelous deeds. You watch over me in everything I do. I will exalt You and praise Your holy name. I trade in my anxiety for Your perfect peace. I cast all my anxiety on You because You care for me (see 1 Peter 5:7). I am so grateful for Your peace which transcends all understanding (see Philippians 4:7). In the name of Jesus, my Rock and Refuge, I pray. Amen.

Pursuing the Heart of God - Book 2

Day 5 ♥♥ Tired and Weary? Rest in Me

Ask God:

Heavenly Father, why do I wait until I am maxed out physically, emotionally, and spiritually to seek You for renewed strength and increased power? Your Word promises that when I put my hope in You, You will renew my strength. I will soar on wings like eagles, run and not grow weary, walk and not be faint (see Isaiah 40:31). Help me to seek Your guidance and wisdom at the beginning of my trials, before I run out of fuel running in my own direction. Lord, I put my faith in You and Your power within Me, to walk me through this challenge. Lord, what do You want me to hear and know today?

Listen to God - A Message from His Heart:

Come to Me, weary one. Lay down your burdens at My feet. I will carry your heavy load and exchange it for a lighter load to bear. Put your confidence in Me and *find rest for your weary soul. My yoke is easy and My burden is light.* Surrender everything to Me and rest. Leave your worries and your cares in My capable hands. Allow Me to remove the weight of your responsibilities and give you My perfect peace.

Hold fast to Me. Depend on Me for your every need. *When you are weak, it is then you are strong.* Trade in your stress, lay it down, and do not take it up again. Replace it with the confidence and joy of trusting in Me for everything you desire and need. *My joy is your strength.* Take hold of the hope set before you, and be encouraged. This hope in Jesus Christ is *an anchor for the soul, firm and secure.*

When you face trials, consider it pure joy, a testing of your faith. Learn to persevere to the finish to grow in your maturity and faith in Me. I allow you to experience challenges that will increase your faith and cause you to depend on Me in increasing measure.

Do not fear, for I have redeemed you; I have called you by name; you are Mine. When you pass through the waters, I will be with you, and when you pass through the rivers, they will not sweep over you. When you walk through the fire, you will not be burned; the flames will not set you ablaze. I am with you at all times, in all places, leading you through your difficulties and challenges.

Trust Me completely for everything. I am the Sovereign Lord, in control of all things. Submit yourself to Me. *I am your helper. Be not afraid.* I will see you through this difficult time. *Cast all your anxiety on Me because I care for you.* I will take care of you and allow your soul a break from the stress you endure.

Rest in Me. *Be still and know that I am God. Come near to Me, and I will come near to you.* I do not give you more than you can handle. I give generously the power of My Spirit within you. Look within you and find the strength which reinforces your constitution and foundation in Me. I am here. I desire to daily meet with you in a quiet place where I can effectively communicate the depth of My love and concern for you.

You are My beloved child, whom I love. I do not allow you to be overwhelmed when you depend on Me. Rest in Me, My love. I am your safe place. Rest in Me. I am your Shelter and your strong Tower. I will rescue you from your present difficulties in due time. Seek Me in the middle of your storms, and find your respite in Me. I will walk you through the valleys and push the mountains aside that stand in your way. I prepare the path I have marked out for you. *This is the good way. Walk in it and you will find rest for your soul.*

Matthew 11:28-30; 2 Corinthians 12:10; Nehemiah 8:10;
Hebrews 6:19; James 1:2-4; Isaiah 43:1-2; Hebrews 13:6;
1 Peter 5:7; Psalm 46:10; James 4:8; Jeremiah 6:16

Supporting Scripture:

[28]"Come to Me, all you who are weary and burdened, and I will give you rest. [29]Take My yoke upon you and learn from Me; for I am gentle and humble in heart, and you will find rest for your souls. [30]For My yoke is easy and My burden is light."—Matthew 11:28-30

That is why, for Christ's sake, I delight in weaknesses, in insults, in hardships, in persecutions, in difficulties. For when I am weak, then I am strong.—2 Corinthians 12:10

"…the joy of the LORD is your strength."—Nehemiah 8:10

We have this hope as an anchor for the soul, firm and secure.—Hebrews 6:19

[2]Consider it pure joy, my brothers and sisters, whenever you face trials of many kinds, [3]because you know that the testing of your faith produces perseverance. [4]Let perseverance finish its work so that you may be mature and complete, not lacking anything.—James 1:2-4

[1]"Do not fear, for I have redeemed you; I have summoned you by name; you are Mine. [2]When you pass through the waters, I will be with you; and when you pass through the rivers, they will not sweep over you. When you walk through the fire, you will not be burned; the flames will not set you ablaze.—Isaiah 43:1-2

So we say with confidence, "The Lord is my helper; I will not be afraid. What can mere mortals to do me?"—Hebrews 13:6

Cast all your anxiety on Him because He cares for you.—1 Peter 5:7

[10]He says, "Be still and know that I am God; I will be exalted among the nations, I will be exalted in the earth.—Psalm 46:10

Come near to God and He will come near to you...—James 4:8

This is what the LORD says, "Stand at the crossroads and look; ask for the ancient paths, ask where the good way is, and walk in it, and you will find rest for your souls..."—Jeremiah 6:16

Prayer:

Father, thank You for Your comforting, encouraging words and promises. I will find rest for my weary soul when I spend some time alone with You. Jesus, as I draw near to You now, please draw near to Me and quiet me with Your love. Speak to my heart directly from Your heart through the voice of the Holy Spirit within me. Lord, I seek You now, as I silence my heart and mind and reflect on the fact that You are God. In the quietness of this secret place, my innermost thoughts, allow me to clearly hear a word from You. In the name of Jesus, my Rescuer and my Refuge, I pray. Amen.

Personal Reflections:

1) From the **Listen to God** section above, pick out a phrase or two that spoke directly to your heart today. Write the words here:

2) As you re-read and think about the words you wrote above, record any additional words or thoughts that come to your mind:

3) Which of the words or thoughts you recorded above might be from God? Underline or highlight them. Does any Scripture come to mind as you re-read what you've written above? If so, write the portion of Scripture that you recall:

4) Turn to the concordance of your Bible and look up one of the words you recalled from Scripture. Scan the verses cited under the word you have referenced in the concordance and record the references of one or two of the verses that the Holy Spirit illumines with special meaning for you today:

5) Turn to each of the references you recorded above. Read the verse and the surrounding passages. Do any additional words or phrases have special meaning for you today? Perhaps something you needed to hear? Wisdom for a

problem you face? An answer to a question? A timely word for a difficult circumstance you currently navigate? If so, record the Scripture or words here:

6) What further question(s) do you have for God today? Write them here:

7) Seek God for answers to the question(s) you wrote above. Ask God one of the questions, and then, sit quietly and wait for His reply. Record the first thought that enters your mind. Write all the thoughts you have as you sit and listen to the Lord:

8) Chances are good that the thoughts you recorded as you sat quietly waiting for the Lord's response were indeed thoughts whispered to you by the Holy Spirit within you. Re-read the thoughts above and ask God to confirm the thoughts that are from Him. Record any new inspirations you hear in your thoughts now:

Identify the Voice:

Re-read the responses you've written to the previous few questions. Run them through the tests below. In each test, the characteristic of God's voice is listed before the OR and the characteristic of Satan's voice is listed after it. Do those thoughts recorded in the section above:

    a. Align with the character of God OR the ways of Satan?
    b. Agree with the Word of God OR contradict it?
    c. Produce the peace of God in your soul OR stir up strife?
    d. Convict you OR condemn you?
    e. Bring spiritual clarity OR confusion?
    f. Offer the Lord's wisdom, instruction, comfort, and encouragement OR cause you to feel doubt, fear, worry, or shame?
    g. Bring emotional healing OR cause additional emotional pain?

Using the above tests as your guide, draw a line through any thoughts in the previous section that might be from your enemy, the devil. Take a minute to rebuke Satan aloud. Do not believe his lies or buy in to his accusations or condemnations that you identify in your thoughts.

Going Deeper in Two-way Conversation with God:

    1) Father in heaven, You are my Rock and Refuge. Please share Your heart with me now. How do I get to that place of

shelter and rest in You? What do I need to add to or remove from my life to best achieve this? (Write what you hear in your thoughts.)

2) Jesus, my Savior, will You now reveal the desires of Your heart for me? How do I weather this storm and maintain a resilient spirit and faith? (Record His words and ideas for you.)

3) Holy Spirit, I tune into Your voice and ask that You would remind me of and direct me to pertinent Scripture right now as we speak. Lord, what do You want me to know from Your Word? (Record all words and passages that come to mind just now.)

Review the thoughts God gave you above. Is there a common theme in the impressions you recorded? Perhaps you heard a word that especially warms your heart today? What Scripture comes to mind as you review your notes? Use the concordance of your Bible to look up a word that especially stood out to you or a word that you heard more than once in your thoughts. Scan the list of occurrences of that word cited in Scripture. When you see a verse in the concordance that has special meaning for you today, the Holy Spirit is highlighting that verse for you. Turn to that passage of Scripture and read it. Write the verse here. Then, write all further insights and confirmations the Holy Spirit gives you as you read and ponder God's Word for you today.

Prayer:

Most High, omnipotent Father, I rejoice in Your sovereign power to demolish all strongholds and restore peace and rest to my soul. Lord, thank You that You walk me through my battles and bring me to a peaceful place of rest in You. Thank You, great Shepherd, that You carry me as a lamb in Your arms, away from dangers, foils, and snares, and lead me to the still waters and lush meadows, Your haven of security and well-being. Lord, please prepare and light the way You have marked out for me, and help me run this race with perseverance, focusing on You only. In the name of Jesus Christ, I pray. Amen.

Pursuing the Heart of God - Book 2

Day 6 ♥♥ Self-Control

Ask God:

Father, at times my life feels so out of control. You know that one of my biggest challenges is surrendering to You, so that Your Spirit can produce in me the fruit of self-control. I confess that I am very weak and immature in this spiritual discipline in my life. I need to recognize that I can do none of this in my own power, but truly, it is a fruit produced by the power of the Holy Spirit when I acknowledge Him and submit to His power within me. It's not whatever I, myself, can or cannot do. It's whatever Your Holy Spirit can do through me. Help me to tap in to this power within me at all times, especially when I feel weak and indulgent. Give me the willpower to yield to Your voice inside me that steers me away from temptation and sin. Holy Spirit, please speak to me about this in our time together today.

Listen to God - A Message from His Heart:

Beloved one, My Son Jesus Christ liberated you from your sin. He has *set you free from the yoke of slavery to sin.* Do not *gratify the desires of the flesh doing whatever you want. Walk in step with the Spirit,* and do not be in conflict with Him. Surrender your sinful nature to Me, and I will produce the fruit of righteousness and self-control in your spirit.

Take delight in the Lord, and He will give you the desires of your heart. Commit your way to the Lord, trust in Him, and He will do this: He will make your righteous reward shine like the dawn, your vindication like the noonday sun. Delight in Me, and though you may stumble, you will not fall. I will *uphold you with My hand.*

When temptation and sin come knocking at your door, do not open it. Deny yourself and stay safely behind the gate of self-control. Do not allow the devil access to your life. *The thief comes only to steal, kill, and destroy. I have come to give you life to the full.* Remain strong in your convictions. Have faith that I can remove all evil strongholds in your life. I will set you free from sin and bondage. *I give release to the prisoners and restore sight to the spiritually blind. I bind up the broken* places in your heart that cause you to crave that which will not bring you true joy and satisfaction.

Pay attention to My voice within. Claim your victory in the name of Jesus Christ, by His shed blood on the cross. He has already conquered sin on your behalf. *You are a new creation. The old has gone; the new is here.* Live anew and enjoy your new life of freedom. Walk in the victory of Christ by *living in step with His Holy Spirit* within you. Maintain your relationship with the Spirit by remaining in continual communication with Him. Do not pretend to be deaf to His voice. Listen and obey; you will receive your reward, and it will be worth so much more than the momentary indulgence and pleasure of disobedience.

Galatians 5:1; Galatians 5:16-17; Psalm 37:4-6;
Psalm 37:23-24; John 10:10; Isaiah 61:1;
2 Corinthians 5:17; Galatians 5:25

Supporting Scripture:

It is for freedom that Christ has set us free. Stand firm, then, and do not let yourselves be burdened again by a yoke of slavery.—Galatians 5:1

[16]So I say, walk by the Spirit, and you will not gratify the desires of the flesh. [17]The flesh desires what is contrary to the Spirit, and the Spirit what is contrary to the flesh. They are in conflict with each

other, so that you are not to do whatever you want.—Galatians 5:16-17

[4]Take delight in the LORD and He will give you the desires of your heart. [5]Commit your way to the LORD, trust in Him and He will do this: [6]He will make your righteous reward shine like the dawn, your vindication like the noonday sun.—Psalm 37:4-6

[23]The LORD makes firm the steps of the one who delights in Him; [24]though he may stumble, he will not fall, for the LORD upholds him with His hand.—Psalm 37:23-24

"The thief comes only to steal and kill and destroy; I have come that they may have life, and have it to the full."—John 10:10

"The Spirit of the Sovereign Lord is on Me, because the Lord has anointed Me to proclaim good news to the poor. He has sent Me to bind up the brokenhearted, to proclaim freedom for the captives and release from darkness for the prisoners."—Isaiah 61:1

Therefore, if anyone is in Christ, the new creation has come: The old has gone, the new is here!—2 Corinthians 5:17

Since we live by the Spirit, let us keep in step with the Spirit.—Galatians 5:25

Prayer:

Holy Spirit, help me be more dependent on You to produce in me the fruit of self-control. I can do none of this in my own strength and power. I have no power of my own. My spirit is willing, but my flesh is weak. Strengthen me and empower me to live according to Your good, pleasing, and perfect will. I confess my sin and repent of it as I walk away from the desires of the flesh that try to hold me captive. I claim freedom in the blood of Christ and His death on the cross. He already won the victory and holds the keys to sin, death, and the grave. I died with Jesus, and now He lives in Me and through Me, by His Spirit. Jesus is risen, and I am seated with Him in the heavenly realms. I am a new creation in Jesus Christ (see 2 Corinthians 5:17). Spirit of God, show me the person You see when You look at me. Share Your heart with me now as we meet and talk. In Jesus' name I pray. Amen.

Personal Reflections:

1) From the **Listen to God** section above, pick out a phrase or two that spoke directly to your heart today. Write the words here:

2) As you re-read and think about the words you wrote above, record any additional words or thoughts that come to your mind:

3) Which of the words or thoughts you recorded above might be from God? Underline or highlight them. Does any Scripture come to mind as you re-read what you've written above? If so, write the portion of Scripture that you recall:

4) Turn to the concordance of your Bible and look up one of the words you recalled from Scripture. Scan the verses cited under the word you have referenced in the concordance and record the references of one or two of the verses that the Holy Spirit illumines with special meaning for you today:

5) Turn to each of the references you recorded above. Read the verse and the surrounding passages. Do any additional words or phrases have special meaning for you today? Perhaps something you needed to hear? Wisdom for a problem you face? An answer to a question? A timely word for a difficult circumstance you currently navigate? If so, record the Scripture or words here:

6) What further question(s) do you have for God today? Write them here:

7) Seek God for answers to the question(s) you wrote above. Ask God one of the questions, and then, sit quietly and wait for His reply. Record the first thought that enters your mind. Write all the thoughts you have as you sit and listen to the Lord:

8) Chances are good that the thoughts you recorded as you sat quietly waiting for the Lord's response were indeed thoughts whispered to you by the Holy Spirit within you. Re-read the thoughts above and ask God to confirm the thoughts that are from Him. Record any new inspirations you hear in your thoughts now:

Identify the Voice:

Re-read the responses you've written to the previous few questions. Run them through the tests below. In each test, the characteristic of God's voice is listed before the OR and the characteristic of Satan's voice is listed after it. Do those thoughts recorded in the section above:

a. Align with the character of God OR the ways of Satan?
b. Agree with the Word of God OR contradict it?
c. Produce the peace of God in your soul OR stir up strife?
d. Convict you OR condemn you?
e. Bring spiritual clarity OR confusion?
f. Offer the Lord's wisdom, instruction, comfort, and encouragement OR cause you to feel doubt, fear, worry, or shame?
g. Bring emotional healing OR cause additional emotional pain?

Using the above tests as your guide, draw a line through any thoughts in the previous section that might be from your enemy, the devil. Take a minute to rebuke Satan aloud. Do not believe his lies or buy in to his accusations or condemnations that you identify in your thoughts.

Going Deeper in Two-way Conversation with God:

1) Righteous Father, please help me understand the importance of submitting myself to the control and empowerment of the Holy Spirit. (Record all His words and thoughts to you.)

2) Jesus, my Friend, teach me how to remain in step with the Spirit and renounce temptation and sin. Then give me the strong conviction and desire to do this. (Write the ideas and impressions He gives you.)

3) Holy Spirit, give me the ability to pay attention to Your voice with my obedience to Your instructions. Open my ears to hear You, and give me the desire to be obedient. Impress on me the reason I need to submit myself to Your leading and direction. (Journal every word and thought you receive.)

Review the thoughts God gave you above. Is there a common theme in the impressions you recorded? Perhaps you heard a word that especially warms your heart today? What Scripture comes to mind as you review your notes? Use the concordance of your Bible to look up a word that especially stood out to you or a word that you heard more than once in your thoughts. Scan the list of occurrences of that word cited in Scripture. When you see a verse in the concordance that has special meaning for you today, the Holy Spirit is highlighting that verse for you. Turn to that passage of Scripture and read it. Write the verse here. Then, write all further insights and confirmations the Holy Spirit gives you as you read and ponder God's Word for you today.

Prayer:

God, thank You for sharing Your heart with me now. Father, help me to not focus on myself and my power but to fully rely on You and Your power to provide me an escape when I am tempted to exercise a lack of self-control. Spirit, produce in me the fruit of self-control, so that I may display the righteousness of a life surrendered to You. Lord, I yield my heart and will to You now. I ask You to remove all ungodly pleasures and strongholds in my life. Forgive me when I am weak; when I stumble, do not let me fall. Thank You for Your grace and mercy to me. As the Holy Spirit sanctifies me, teach me to be more grace-filled and merciful toward others. I ask this in the name of Jesus Christ, my Lord. Amen.

Pursuing the Heart of God - Book 2

Day 7 ♥♥ Be Armed for Spiritual Battle

Ask God:

Lord, sometimes I can really relate to what Paul said in Romans 7:15: "I do not understand what I do. For what I want to do I do not do, but what I hate I do." Why do I continue to behave and respond in the flesh when You have given me new life in the Spirit? What is this battle raging within me that keeps me from living the sanctified life You intended for me? Lord, I confess my sin and ask that You would help me fight this battle and win.

Listen to God - A Message from His Heart:

My child, it is good for you to realize that you are involved in a form of daily spiritual battle between the flesh and the Spirit. Use the Holy Spirit's power to annihilate the force of sin in your life. Sin has no control over you, unless you allow it to. *You are no longer a slave to sin, but a child of God.*

You are a new creation in Christ Jesus. You have the same mighty power living in you that was exerted when God raised Jesus Christ from the dead. The Holy Spirit is your ally and defender. You may exercise His supernatural strength in all your encounters. I am your Warrior God; I help you fight your battles and win them!

Also understand that you live in continual spiritual warfare of good vs. evil. Every morning, dress yourself for spiritual battle by putting on *the full armor of God, so that you will be able to stand your ground.* Gird your waist with the *belt of truth*, claiming who you are in Christ; you are supernaturally empowered by the indwelling Holy Spirit. With the *helmet of salvation*, you put on the mind of Christ, giving you wisdom and discernment with regard to your enemy and his attacks. Secure the *breastplate of righteousness* in place to protect your heart and defend your birthright as a child of God. Hold up the *shield of faith, with which you can extinguish all the flaming arrows of the evil one. Stand firm with your feet fitted with the sandals of the gospel of peace.* Take up and carry the *sword of the Spirit, which is the Word of God,* so you can fight against the enemy's lies with the truth of Scripture and God's promises. *Pray in the Spirit on all occasions with all kinds of prayers and requests. Always be alert and keep on praying for all God's people.*

Draw on the dynamic power of the Holy Spirit whenever you find yourself in a diabolical battle. Your enemy's attacks may be subtle. Sometimes you do not even know you are in a fight until you have lost the battle. Remain alert to the devil's ways, knowing that he will first go after your weakest areas. *Our struggle is not against flesh and blood, but against the rulers, against the authorities, against the powers of this dark world and against the spiritual forces of evil in the heavenly realms.*

When you are in a struggle against another human, consider the provocative nature of the evil one. Often times, he is your true opponent. *Your enemy the devil prowls around like a roaring lion looking for someone to devour.* Do not fall prey to his devious schemes. *Be strong in the Lord and in His mighty power. Live as wise, not as unwise.* Remember that Christ has already defeated Satan, sin, death, and the grave. Do not give the devil more power than he is due. Christ has made him powerless. Claim your victory over evil and the evil one, by the shed blood of Jesus on the cross. You are victorious in Jesus Christ. Stand firm and win over evil. You are armed with power from on high, through the Holy Spirit and the sword of the Spirit. I have given you authority *to overcome all the power of the enemy.* Believe it! Claim it! Live it!

Galatians 4:6-7; 2 Corinthians 5:17;
Ephesians 1:19-20; Ephesians 6:10-18;
1 Peter 5:8-9; Ephesians 5:15; Luke 10:19

Supporting Scripture:

[6]Because you are His sons, God sent the Spirit of His Son into our hearts, the Spirit Who calls out, "*Abba*, Father." [7]So you are no longer a slave, but God's child; and since you are His child, God has made you also an heir.—Galatians 4:6-7

Therefore, if anyone is in Christ, the new creation has come: The old has gone, the new is here!—2 Corinthians 5:17

[19]…and His incomparably great power for us who believe. That power is the same as the mighty strength [20]He exerted when He raised Christ from the dead and seated Him at His right hand in the heavenly realms.—Ephesians 1:19-20

The Armor of God [10]Finally, be strong in the Lord and in His mighty power. [11]Put on the full armor of God, so that you can take your stand against the devil's schemes. [12]For our struggle is not against flesh and blood, but against the rulers, against the authorities, against the powers of this dark world and against the spiritual forces of evil in the heavenly realms. [13]Therefore put on the full armor of God, so that when the day of evil comes, you may be able to stand your ground, and after you have done everything to stand. [14]Stand firm then, with the belt of truth buckled around your waist, with the breastplate of righteousness in place, [15]and with your feet fitted with the readiness that comes from the gospel of peace. [16]In addition to all this, take up the shield of faith with which you can extinguish all the flaming arrows of the evil one. [17]Take the helmet of salvation and the sword of the Spirit, which is the Word of God. [18]And pray in the Spirit on all occasions with all kinds of prayers and requests. With this in mind, be alert and always keep on praying for all the Lord's people.—Ephesians 6:10-18

[8]Be alert and of sober mind. Your enemy the devil prowls around like a roaring lion looking for someone to devour. [9]Resist him, standing firm in the faith, because you know that the family of

believers throughout the world is undergoing the same kind of sufferings. —1 Peter 5:8-9

Be very careful, then, how you live—not as unwise but as wise— Ephesians 5:15

I have given you authority to trample on snakes and scorpions and to overcome all the power of the enemy; nothing will harm you."— Luke 10:19

Prayer:

Dear Jesus, thank You for shedding Your blood on the cross and claiming Your victory over sin, death, and the grave. Thank You for providing me that same victory, as well as the power and authority over all evil and the evil one. I am so grateful that I do not stand alone to battle the forces of evil, but You stand at my side. You are my Warrior God, hiding me in the shadow of Your wings (see Psalm 17:8) and protecting me from my enemies. Lord, thank You for providing me the Armor of God, so that I may stand firm in battle and remain standing (see Ephesians 6:13). Thank You for the victory and for the supernatural power of the Holy Spirit dwelling in me. Please help me be alert to the ways of the enemy and engage in battle with the armor, the weapons, and the authority You provide. Holy Spirit, please speak to me now and share Your wisdom with me to better prepare me for anything the enemy throws my way. In the name of Jesus Christ, I pray. Amen.

Personal Reflections:

1) From the **Listen to God** section above, pick out a phrase or two that spoke directly to your heart today. Write the words here:

2) As you re-read and think about the words you wrote above, record any additional words or thoughts that come to your mind:

3) Which of the words or thoughts you recorded above might be from God? Underline or highlight them. Does any Scripture come to mind as you re-read what you've written above? If so, write the portion of Scripture that you recall:

4) Turn to the concordance of your Bible and look up one of the words you recalled from Scripture. Scan the verses cited under the word you have referenced in the concordance and record the references of one or two of the verses that the Holy Spirit illumines with special meaning for you today:

5) Turn to each of the references you recorded above. Read the verse and the surrounding passages. Do any additional words or phrases have special meaning for you today?

Perhaps something you needed to hear? Wisdom for a problem you face? An answer to a question? A timely word for a difficult circumstance you currently navigate? If so, record the Scripture or words here:

6) What further question(s) do you have for God today? Write them here:

7) Seek God for answers to the question(s) you wrote above. Ask God one of the questions, and then, sit quietly and wait for His reply. Record the first thought that enters your mind. Write all the thoughts you have as you sit and listen to the Lord:

8) Chances are good that the thoughts you recorded as you sat quietly waiting for the Lord's response were indeed thoughts whispered to you by the Holy Spirit within you. Re-read the thoughts above and ask God to confirm the thoughts that are from Him. Record any new inspirations you hear in your thoughts now:

Identify the Voice:

Re-read the responses you've written to the previous few questions. Run them through the tests below. In each test, the characteristic of God's voice is listed before the OR and the characteristic of Satan's voice is listed after it. Do those thoughts recorded in the section above:

    a. Align with the character of God OR the ways of Satan?
    b. Agree with the Word of God OR contradict it?
    c. Produce the peace of God in your soul OR stir up strife?
    d. Convict you OR condemn you?
    e. Bring spiritual clarity OR confusion?
    f. Offer the Lord's wisdom, instruction, comfort, and encouragement OR cause you to feel doubt, fear, worry, or shame?
    g. Bring emotional healing OR cause additional emotional pain?

Using the above tests as your guide, draw a line through any thoughts in the previous section that might be from your enemy, the devil. Take a minute to rebuke Satan aloud. Do not believe his lies or buy in to his accusations or condemnations that you identify in your thoughts.

Going Deeper in Two-way Conversation with God:

    1) Loving Father, please expose the broken places in my heart and show me the areas of weakness that the enemy will

most certainly go after. (Record all thoughts that come to mind in this moment.)

2) Jesus, my Victor, please enlighten me to the truth about my vulnerabilities. Replace the lies of the enemy with Your truth. Tell me how to defend myself against the enemy's attacks in these areas. (Write down all thoughts, ideas, and Scripture verses that come to mind right now.)

3) Holy Spirit, please help me be alert to Satan and his ways. Remind me that I struggle not with flesh and blood but against the evil one. Empower me with the sword of the Spirit, the Word of God, to fight these attacks. Please give me verses that will combat the enemy when he strikes my weak spots. (Journal all His words and the verses He leads you to for this application.)

Review the thoughts God gave you above. Is there a common theme in the impressions you recorded? Perhaps you heard a word that especially warms your heart today? What Scripture comes to mind as you review your notes? Use the concordance of your Bible to look up a word that especially stood out to you or a word that you heard more than once in your thoughts. Scan the list of occurrences of that word cited in Scripture. When you see a verse in the concordance that has special meaning for you today, the Holy Spirit is highlighting that verse for you. Turn to that passage of Scripture and read it. Write the verse here. Then, write all further insights and confirmations the Holy Spirit gives you as you read and ponder God's Word for you today.

Prayer:

Holy Spirit, thank You for sharing with me God's wisdom, words, power, and protection as I fight these daily battles. Spirit, I ask that You will daily empower me with Your wisdom and Your Word. My Helper, please teach me to always remain alert to the enemy's ways and recognize each battle I engage in for what it truly is. I claim my victory in Jesus. I claim all power and authority over evil and the evil one in the name of Jesus Christ and by His blood. Thank You, Lord. Amen.

Pursuing the Heart of God - Book 2

Day 8 ♥♥ Be Joyful

Ask God:

Dearest Father, You knit me together in the womb, and You know my inmost being (see Psalm 139:13). You know that I am not naturally a happy, joyful person. However, I do understand and believe that true joy is not a feeling; instead, it is a gift from the Spirit and a confidence I experience in my relationship with You. Your joy is my inner strength (see Nehemiah 8:10). My joy is made complete in a close connection and daily conversation with You. Thank You for producing joy in my life through the gift of the Holy Spirit within me. Listening to Your voice and reading Your Word both bring me great and lasting joy. Holy Spirit, please share Your insights with me today.

Listen to God - A Message from His Heart:

My child, you may not feel joyful; however, that is exactly what you are. You experience supernatural joy through the gift of My Spirit. You possess the confidence in knowing that I am your God, I am in control, and you can place your hope and trust in Me and My promises. You have the assurance that I love you and care for you; therefore, *in all things I work for your good.*

We are not speaking about the happiness that good circumstances produce but an inner, enduring joy that supersedes the pleasures that the world offers. You may remain joyful in every situation because of your relationship with Jesus Christ, Who sustains you. That relationship never changes. *Jesus is the same yesterday, today, and forever.*

I am your Strength and Shield. When your heart trusts in Me, it leaps for joy. I grant you *unending blessings with the joy of My presence. My joy is your strength.* I turn your *crying into dancing and your mourning into joy.* Rejoice and be glad that My Spirit gives you unending peace and lasting joy.

My peace and joy are available to you in good times and bad through the gift of the Spirit. You may rejoice even when I don't deliver you from your troubles, because you know that I will take care of you and provide for all your needs. It is during your trials that you grow the most. You learn to depend on Me and know that *I will never leave you or forget about you.*

Joy is also a choice. You may enjoy a positive outlook as you focus on Me rather than your sorrows and difficult circumstances. You know I will walk you through your trials. I am in control of everything. *Nothing will separate you from My love.* Be thankful for what I am doing in you through your challenges. *When you are weak, I am your strength.* Your joy will be made full. Choose Me and be joyful.

Psalm 139:13; Nehemiah 8:10; Romans 8:28;
Hebrews 13:8; Psalm 28:7; Psalm 21:6; Psalm 30:11;
Hebrews 13:5; Romans 8:38-39; 2 Corinthians 12:10

Supporting Scripture:

For you created my inmost being; you knit me together in my mother's womb.—Psalm 139:13

Nehemiah said, "Go and enjoy choice food and sweet drinks, and send some to those who have nothing prepared. This day is holy to our Lord. Do not grieve, for the joy of the LORD is your strength."—Nehemiah 8:10

And we know that in all things God works for the good of those who love Him, who have been called according to His purpose.—Romans 8:28

Jesus Christ is the same yesterday and today and forever.—Hebrews 13:8

The LORD is my strength and my shield; my heart trusts in Him, and He helps me. My heart leaps for joy, and with my song I praise Him.—Psalm 28:7

Surely You have granted him unending blessings and made him glad with the joy of Your presence.—Psalm 21:6

You turned my wailing into dancing; You removed my sackcloth and clothed me with joy.—Psalm 30:11

…"Never will I leave you; never will I forsake you."—Hebrews 13:5

[38]For I am convinced that neither death nor life, neither angels nor demons, neither the present nor the future, nor any powers, [39]neither height nor depth, nor anything else in all creation, will be able to separate us from the love of God that is in Christ Jesus our Lord.—Romans 8:38-39

That is why, for Christ's sake, I delight in weaknesses, in insults, in hardships, in persecutions, in difficulties. For when I am weak, then I am strong.—2 Corinthians 12:10

Prayer:

Dear Most High God, I am joyful because of the peace, hope, faith, and confidence I have in knowing You love me and You are in control of all things. There is no one like You, Lord. There is no place I'd rather be than spending time in relationship with You. It brings me great joy to listen to Your voice and read about You in Your Word. Thank You for adopting me as Your child and allowing me to approach You with freedom and confidence. Holy

Spirit, magnify my joy by allowing me to clearly hear Your voice and Your words for me in this moment as we sit in conversation. In the name of Jesus Christ, I pray. Amen.

Personal Reflections:

1) From the **Listen to God** section above, pick out a phrase or two that spoke directly to your heart today. Write the words here:

2) As you re-read and think about the words you wrote above, record any additional words or thoughts that come to your mind:

3) Which of the words or thoughts you recorded above might be from God? Underline or highlight them. Does any Scripture come to mind as you re-read what you've written above? If so, write the portion of Scripture that you recall:

4) Turn to the concordance of your Bible and look up one of the words you recalled from Scripture. Scan the verses cited under the word you have referenced in the concordance and record the references of one or two of the verses that the Holy Spirit illumines with special meaning for you today:

5) Turn to each of the references you recorded above. Read the verse and the surrounding passages. Do any additional words or phrases have special meaning for you today? Perhaps something you needed to hear? Wisdom for a problem you face? An answer to a question? A timely word for a difficult circumstance you currently navigate? If so, record the Scripture or words here:

6) What further question(s) do you have for God today? Write them here:

7) Seek God for answers to the question(s) you wrote above. Ask God one of the questions, and then, sit quietly and wait for His reply. Record the first thought that enters your mind. Write all the thoughts you have as you sit and listen to the Lord:

8) Chances are good that the thoughts you recorded as you sat quietly waiting for the Lord's response were indeed thoughts whispered to you by the Holy Spirit within you. Re-read the thoughts above and ask God to confirm the thoughts that are from Him. Record any new inspirations you hear in your thoughts now:

Identify the Voice:

Re-read the responses you've written to the previous few questions. Run them through the tests below. In each test, the characteristic of God's voice is listed before the OR and the characteristic of Satan's voice is listed after it. Do those thoughts recorded in the section above:

    a. Align with the character of God OR the ways of Satan?
    b. Agree with the Word of God OR contradict it?
    c. Produce the peace of God in your soul OR stir up strife?
    d. Convict you OR condemn you?

e. Bring spiritual clarity OR confusion?
f. Offer the Lord's wisdom, instruction, comfort, and encouragement OR cause you to feel doubt, fear, worry, or shame?
g. Bring emotional healing OR cause additional emotional pain?

Using the above tests as your guide, draw a line through any thoughts in the previous section that might be from your enemy, the devil. Take a minute to rebuke Satan aloud. Do not believe his lies or buy in to his accusations or condemnations that you identify in your thoughts.

Going Deeper in Two-way Conversation with God:

1) Father God, what brings You the most joy? (Record what you hear from Him.)

2) Jesus, my Savior, please explain to me the joy You anticipated even in Your darkest hour, as stated in Hebrews 12:2: "fixing our eyes on Jesus, the pioneer and perfecter of faith. For the joy set before Him He endured the cross, scorning its shame, and sat down at the right hand of the throne of God." (Write everything He brings to your mind right now.)

3) Holy Spirit, please sanctify me to become more like Christ, and produce in me the fruit of joy. Show me what that will require. (Journal all your thoughts and ideas.)

Review the thoughts God gave you above. Is there a common theme in the impressions you recorded? Perhaps you heard a word that especially warms your heart today? What Scripture comes to mind as you review your notes? Use the concordance of your Bible to look up a word that especially stood out to you or a word that you heard more than once in your thoughts. Scan the list of occurrences of that word cited in Scripture. When you see a verse in the concordance that has special meaning for you today, the Holy Spirit is highlighting that verse for you. Turn to that passage of Scripture and read it. Write the verse here. Then, write all further insights and confirmations the Holy Spirit gives you as you read and ponder God's Word for you today.

Prayer:

Lord, I can really relate to David's claim in Psalm 30:11: "You turned my wailing into dancing; You removed my sackcloth and clothed me with joy." I experienced that new joy as You brought me from depression to dancing, and now I cannot keep silent about Your goodness. You have done wonderful things for me, and I am filled with joy. I see where the Spirit has produced that fruit of joy in me. I will praise You forever, O Lord, my God. My heart sings and leaps for joy, even in the difficult times, because I put my faith and trust in You to carry me through. I can experience joy in any situation. Thank You for this realization. Thank You for Your mercy and grace, peace and joy, love and provision. Thank You for building a firm foundation of joy in my life and a lasting joy in my heart for You. In Jesus' name I pray. Amen.

Pursuing the Heart of God - Book 2

Day 9 ♥♥ Faith as Small as a Mustard Seed

Ask God:

Lord, as with everything, one's faith is tested in trials and strengthened in a relationship with You. Extreme faith is a gift from the Spirit. And yet Your Word promises it takes only a small amount of faith to do great things. Hardships test the faith and produce perseverance. Is it even possible to increase my faith without the trials? Either way, I have faith in Your promise that in all things You work for the good of those who love You and are called according to Your purpose (see Romans 8:28).

Listen to God - A Message from His Heart:

My beloved friend, when you encounter hardship, exercise your faith. It takes only a speck of faith to accomplish great things. *Truly I tell you, if you have faith as small as a mustard seed, you can say to this mountain, "Move from here to there." And it will move. Nothing will be impossible for you.* Even a little faith can move mountains.

Truly I tell you, if you have faith and do not doubt, you can say to this mountain, "Go, throw yourself into the sea," and it will be done. If you believe, you will receive whatever you ask for in prayer. Have faith and do not doubt. *When you doubt, you are as a wave on the sea, tossed back and forth, double-minded. You should not expect to receive anything you ask for.*

Consider it pure joy whenever you face trials of many kinds, because you know that the testing of your faith produces perseverance. Let perseverance finish its work so that you may be mature and complete, not lacking anything. Faith and trust go hand in hand. *Trust in Me with all your heart, and lean not on your own understanding; in all your ways, submit to Me, and I will make your paths straight.* Listen to My voice and submit yourself to Me. Trust that I am in control of all things; have faith that I will give you anything you ask for in My name.

Faith is a gift from Me. *You have been saved through faith by My grace,* and you live by faith every day. There are different kinds of faith. Extreme *faith is a gift of the Spirit.* Your faith will make you well. When you ask for healing, believe in it! *Whatever you ask for in prayer, believe that you have received it, and it will be yours. Nothing is impossible when you believe.* Jesus dwells in your heart through faith. He is able to do *immeasurably more than all you ask or imagine, according to His power that is at work within you.* Have faith and believe it!

When you experience a breakdown in your faith, do not focus on the obstacle in front of you, but *fix your eyes upon Jesus.* Do not grow weary and lose heart. *Do not fix your eyes on what is seen but on what is unseen, since what is seen is temporary, but what is unseen is eternal.* There is but One Who remains in control of all things; it is I, the Sovereign God, Who reigns on high and rules all things and all people at all times. I am trustworthy. I never change. Put your faith and trust in Me; *I AM.*

Always remember *never will I leave you, never will I forsake you.* I love you deeply and want what is best for you. I am always at work behind the scenes. I created you for a purpose; *I have plans for you,* and I desire to share them with you, and lead you down the path I have marked out for you.

You are my beloved child, and I care for you deeply. I desire that you mature in your faith, even if it involves allowing you to endure difficult times to do so. Stand firm in your faith; I will provide the strength and hope to persevere. I know what is best for you, and I will see you through your challenges. Have faith, even as small as a mustard seed!

Matthew 17:20; Matthew 21:21-22; James 1:6-7; James 1:2-4;
Proverbs 3:5-6; Ephesians 2:8; 1 Corinthians 12:8-9; Mark 11:24;
Matthew 17:20; Ephesians 3:20; 2 Corinthians 4:18;
Exodus 3:14; Hebrews 13:5; Jeremiah 29:11

Supporting Scripture:

He replied, "Because you have so little faith. Truly I tell you, if you have faith as small as a mustard seed, you can say to this mountain, 'Move from here to there,' and it will move. Nothing will be impossible for you."—Matthew 17:20

[21]Jesus replied, "Truly I tell you, if you have faith and do not doubt, not only can you do what was done to the fig tree, but also you can say to this mountain, 'Go, throw yourself into the sea,' and it will be done. [22]If you believe, you will receive whatever you ask for in prayer."—Matthew 21:21-22

[6]But when you ask, you must believe and not doubt, because the one who doubts is like a wave of the sea, blown and tossed by the wind. [7]That person should not expect to receive anything from the Lord.—James 1:6-7

[2]Consider it pure joy, my brothers and sisters, whenever you face trials of many kinds, [3]because you know that the testing of your faith produces perseverance. [4]Let perseverance finish its work so that you may be mature and complete, not lacking anything.—James 1:2-4

[5]Trust in the LORD with all your heart and lean not on your own understanding; [6]in all your ways submit to Him and He will make your paths straight.—Proverbs 3:5-6

For it is by grace you have been saved, through faith—and this is not from yourselves, it is the gift of God.—Ephesians 2:8

[8]To one there is given through the Spirit a message of wisdom, to another a message of knowledge by means of the same Spirit, [9]to another faith by the same Spirit, to another gifts of healing by that one Spirit.—1 Corinthians 12:8-9

"Therefore I tell you, whatever you ask for in prayer, believe that you have received it, and it will be yours."—Mark 11:24

He replied, "Because you have so little faith. Truly I tell you, if you have faith as small as a mustard seed, you can say to this mountain, 'Move from here to there,' and it will move. Nothing will be impossible for you."—Matthew 17:20

Now to Him Who is able to do immeasurably more than all we ask or imagine, according to His power that is at work within us,—Ephesians 3:20

So we fix our eyes not on what is seen, but on what is unseen, since what is seen is temporary, but what is unseen is eternal.—2 Corinthians 4:18

God said to Moses, "I AM WHO I AM. This is what you are to say to the Israelites: 'I AM has sent me to you.'"—Exodus 3:14

…"Never will I leave you; never will I forsake you."—Hebrews 13:5

"For I know the plans I have for you," declares the LORD, "plans to prosper you and not to harm you, plans to give you hope and a future."—Jeremiah 29:11

Prayer:

Father in heaven, thank You for the gift of faith, even though it may be small. Thank You that even a speck of faith can move mountains. You are an awesome, all-powerful God, Who works through Your weakest people to show Your greatest strength and power. Almighty God, will You meet with me now, through the Holy Spirit, and increase my faith and trust in You? Work Your grace and Your power in my life. Give me the confidence I need to trust in You wholeheartedly. In Jesus' name I pray. Amen.

Personal Reflections:

1) From the **Listen to God** section above, pick out a phrase or two that spoke directly to your heart today. Write the words here:

2) As you re-read and think about the words you wrote above, record any additional words or thoughts that come to your mind:

3) Which of the words or thoughts you recorded above might be from God? Underline or highlight them. Does any Scripture come to mind as you re-read what you've written above? If so, write the portion of Scripture that you recall:

4) Turn to the concordance of your Bible and look up one of the words you recalled from Scripture. Scan the verses cited under the word you have referenced in the concordance and record the references of one or two of the verses that the Holy Spirit illumines with special meaning for you today:

5) Turn to each of the references you recorded above. Read the verse and the surrounding passages. Do any additional words or phrases have special meaning for you today? Perhaps something you needed to hear? Wisdom for a problem you face? An answer to a question? A timely word for a difficult circumstance you currently navigate? If so, record the Scripture or words here:

6) What further question(s) do you have for God today? Write them here:

7) Seek God for answers to the question(s) you wrote above. Ask God one of the questions, and then, sit quietly and wait for His reply. Record the first thought that enters your mind. Write all the thoughts you have as you sit and listen to the Lord:

8) Chances are good that the thoughts you recorded as you sat quietly waiting for the Lord's response were indeed thoughts whispered to you by the Holy Spirit within you. Re-read the thoughts above and ask God to confirm the thoughts that are from Him. Record any new inspirations you hear in your thoughts now:

Identify the Voice:

Re-read the responses you've written to the previous few questions. Run them through the tests below. In each test, the characteristic of God's voice is listed before the OR and the characteristic of Satan's voice is listed after it. Do those thoughts recorded in the section above:

    a. Align with the character of God OR the ways of Satan?
    b. Agree with the Word of God OR contradict it?
    c. Produce the peace of God in your soul OR stir up strife?
    d. Convict you OR condemn you?
    e. Bring spiritual clarity OR confusion?
    f. Offer the Lord's wisdom, instruction, comfort, and encouragement OR cause you to feel doubt, fear, worry, or shame?
    g. Bring emotional healing OR cause additional emotional pain?

Using the above tests as your guide, draw a line through any thoughts in the previous section that might be from your enemy, the devil. Take a minute to rebuke Satan aloud. Do not believe his lies or buy in to his accusations or condemnations that you identify in your thoughts.

Going Deeper in Two-way Conversation with God:

    1) Father God, please share with me how my faith in You works to move mountains. (Record every word and thought He gives you.)

2) Jesus, my Lord, I want to have the faith like the woman who touched Your robe to be healed. Teach me how to have that kind of faith. What must I do? (Write down all thoughts and ideas Jesus gives you in this moment.)

3) Holy Spirit, please give me the gift of faith. I want to believe and not doubt. Help me overcome my doubt. Please give to me as You determine. What might that be? (Journal the thoughts and verses the Holy Spirit gives you.)

Review the thoughts God gave you above. Is there a common theme in the impressions you recorded? Perhaps you heard a word that especially warms your heart today? What Scripture comes to mind as you review your notes? Use the concordance of your Bible to look up a word that especially stood out to you or a word that you heard more than once in your thoughts. Scan the list of occurrences of that word cited in Scripture. When you see a verse

in the concordance that has special meaning for you today, the Holy Spirit is highlighting that verse for you. Turn to that passage of Scripture and read it. Write the verse here. Then, write all further insights and confirmations the Holy Spirit gives you as you read and ponder God's Word for you today.

Prayer:

Dear Father God, I am grateful for this conversation that we shared today. Thank You for sharing Your heart on the subject of my faith. Holy Spirit, strengthen me with Your gift of faith and empower me to trust in You completely for all things. Father, I am so blessed that You call me Your child, You love me beyond my comprehension, and You know what is best for me and carry it out according to Your good and perfect will. Thank You for Your love and faithfulness to all generations of those who love You. In Jesus' precious name I pray. Amen.

Pursuing the Heart of God - Book 2

Day 10 ♥♥ Praise Him in the Storms

Ask God:

Lord, where have You been during the storms of my life?

Listen to God - A Message from His Heart:

My child, I am with you through each storm in your life, you just don't always know it.

The raindrops that fall during your storms are My tears falling to the earth. I cry with you each time you cry. The lightning that you see flash across the dark sky of your storms is from My heart breaking in two for you. My heart aches for you each time I see you suffer through trials and tribulations. The thunder you hear during your storms is from My anger. I am angry when the people I have created cause you hurt and pain. I am angry when the enemy attacks you and wounds you.

The winds that blow through your storms are the breaths of My sighs moving through the earth. I sigh with compassion when I think of My beloved children going through the pain of daily struggles with relationships, disease, divorce, sin, and death. When the waves on the seas crash against your boat and toss it to and fro in your storms, I am there to make sure the waves are not bigger than your vessel can handle. My hand is upon you.

When you feel you can't last another day, I allow you to rest in my arms, and I *renew your strength*. When you wonder and ask why I would allow you to go through these storms, I do not get angry. It has not been easy for Me to watch you go through these tough times. You're My child and I love you. I want to rescue you from each storm. But in My infinite wisdom, I allow you to endure the pain and suffering to bring you closer to Me. I want to build your character and mature your faith so that I may use you to help others through their storms.

It is during these storms that I hope you will realize how much you need Me. I am waiting for you to cry out to Me so that I can extend My grace to you. *My grace is sufficient for you.* I will pull you through. I am also waiting for you to seek help from others so that I can use them to be like Christ to you. Let down the walls of pride and reach out for assistance.

It is during these times that I hope you'll turn to Me. My heart breaks when My people turn to other things to comfort themselves, like food, alcohol, drugs, gambling, sex, money, and material possessions. I want to be your God, your one and only God. I am your Anchor of hope in the storm. *I am your Stronghold, your Rock and Refuge.* Take your shelter *in the shadow of My wings.* I will protect you from all evil and the evil one.

It is during these storms that I am waiting to show you how much you mean to Me and Whom I can be to you, but sometimes you don't allow Me to do so. You don't give Me the time with you I need to accomplish this, or your pride gets in the way. You want to be so independent and in control of your own life. You want to get yourself out of your own messes in your own way. You run ahead of Me. You do not want to rely on Me or on the fellowship of believers to help you get through the tough times.

In My Word, I tell you how I feel about pride. I hate pride. *Pride comes before a fall. With pride comes disgrace, but with humility comes wisdom. I oppose the proud but give grace to the humble.* When you are weak, it is then that I show My power in you. When you share your needs with Me and with My faithful ones, you are revealing not your weakness but your strength. By asking for help and prayers, you are being humble, so that you may experience all My grace and all My wisdom. But when you try to do it all on your own, you leave Me no room to help.

Do not forsake Me, for *I will never leave you nor forsake you*. I have proven that. I am the God Who saved Noah from the flood. I saved the three Hebrew boys from the fiery furnace. I saved Daniel from the mouths of hungry lions. I was with David when he fought the giant. I released Joseph from Pharaoh's prison. I saved Isaac from being sacrificed on the altar. I delivered Jonah from the belly of the fish. And I will see you through your storms, too. Please notice that I did not keep these people from going through their struggles, but I did not forget about them; I was with them. I allowed them to go through the storms for their good, and then I rescued them. And I will rescue you, too, in My perfect timing, if you will let Me.

Praise Me in the storms. I love you, and I will take care of you. I will *rebuke the wind and the waves*. I do not allow you to endure more than you can handle; however, by the power of My Spirit within, you can handle a lot. Fix your eyes on Me, and I will see you to the end of the storm. *I am with you always, even to the end of the age.* I am with you in every storm. *I set My rainbow in the clouds as My promise to you, that never again will waters become a flood to destroy all life.* You will survive your storms. I will see to it because I love you.

Isaiah 40:31; 2 Corinthians 12:9; 2 Samuel 22:2-3; Psalm 36:7;
Proverbs 16:18; Proverbs 11:2; James 4:6; Hebrews 13:5;
Matthew 8:26; Matthew 28:20; Genesis 9:13-15

Supporting Scripture:

But those who hope in the LORD will renew their strength. They will soar on wings like eagles; they will run and not grow weary, they will walk and not be faint.—Isaiah 40:31

But He said to me, "My grace is sufficient for you, for My power is made perfect in weakness." Therefore I will boast all the more gladly about my weaknesses, so that Christ's power may rest on me.—2 Corinthians 12:9

²He said: "The LORD is my rock, my fortress and my deliverer; ³my God is my rock, in Whom I take refuge, my shield and the horn of my salvation. He is my stronghold, my refuge and my savior—from violent people You save me."—2 Samuel 22:2-3

How priceless is Your unfailing love, O God! People take refuge in the shadow of your wings.—Psalm 36:7

Pride goes before destruction, a haughty spirit before a fall.—Proverbs 16:18

When pride comes, then comes disgrace, but with humility comes wisdom.—Proverbs 11:2

But He gives us more grace. That is why Scripture says: "God opposes the proud but shows favor to the humble."—James 4:6

…"Never will I leave you; never will I forsake you."—Hebrews 13:5

He replied, "You of little faith, why are you so afraid?" Then He got up and rebuked the winds and the waves, and it was completely calm.—Matthew 8:26

"…And surely I am with you always, to the very end of the age."—Matthew 28:20

¹³"I have set my rainbow in the clouds, and it will be the sign of the covenant between Me and the earth. ¹⁴Whenever I bring clouds over the earth and the rainbow appears in the clouds, ¹⁵I will remember My covenant between Me and you and all living creatures of every kind. Never again will the waters become a flood to destroy all life."—Genesis 9:13-15

Prayer:

Lord, I praise You in the storm. I praise You that You do not leave me alone. *"I praise You in Your sanctuary, in Your mighty heavens. I praise You for Your acts of power; for Your surpassing greatness. Let everything that has breath praise the Lord. Praise the Lord"* (see Psalm 150:1-2, 6). With all the breath in me, I praise You, Lord. I praise You because You listen to my cries. Lord, allow me to rest in Your love. Holy Spirit, please allow me to hear some more of Your heart right now. Spirit, speak to me in the stillness of this room as we sit together in conversation. In Jesus' name I pray. Amen.

Personal Reflections:

1) From the **Listen to God** section above, pick out a phrase or two that spoke directly to your heart today. Write the words here:

2) As you re-read and think about the words you wrote above, record any additional words or thoughts that come to your mind:

3) Which of the words or thoughts you recorded above might be from God? Underline or highlight them. Does any Scripture come to mind as you re-read what you've written above? If so, write the portion of Scripture that you recall:

4) Turn to the concordance of your Bible and look up one of the words you recalled from Scripture. Scan the verses cited under the word you have referenced in the concordance and record the references of one or two of the verses that the Holy Spirit illumines with special meaning for you today:

5) Turn to each of the references you recorded above. Read the verse and the surrounding passages. Do any additional words or phrases have special meaning for you today? Perhaps something you needed to hear? Wisdom for a problem you face? An answer to a question? A timely word for a difficult circumstance you currently navigate? If so, record the Scripture or words here:

6) What further question(s) do you have for God today? Write them here:

7) Seek God for answers to the question(s) you wrote above. Ask God one of the questions, and then, sit quietly and wait for His reply. Record the first thought that enters your mind. Write all the thoughts you have as you sit and listen to the Lord:

8) Chances are good that the thoughts you recorded as you sat quietly waiting for the Lord's response were indeed thoughts whispered to you by the Holy Spirit within you. Re-read the thoughts above and ask God to confirm the thoughts that are from Him. Record any new inspirations you hear in your thoughts now:

Identify the Voice:

Re-read the responses you've written to the previous few questions. Run them through the tests below. In each test, the characteristic of God's voice is listed before the OR and the characteristic of Satan's voice is listed after it. Do those thoughts recorded in the section above:

    a. Align with the character of God OR the ways of Satan?
    b. Agree with the Word of God OR contradict it?
    c. Produce the peace of God in your soul OR stir up strife?
    d. Convict you OR condemn you?
    e. Bring spiritual clarity OR confusion?
    f. Offer the Lord's wisdom, instruction, comfort, and encouragement OR cause you to feel doubt, fear, worry, or shame?
    g. Bring emotional healing OR cause additional emotional pain?

Using the above tests as your guide, draw a line through any thoughts in the previous section that might be from your enemy, the devil. Take a minute to rebuke Satan aloud. Do not believe his lies or buy in to his accusations or condemnations that you identify in your thoughts.

Going Deeper in Two-way Conversation with God:

1) Father God, what stirs Your heart into action during my storms? (Record all the thoughts you have.)

2) Jesus, my faithful Savior, thank You for rebuking the wind and waves in my storms and restoring the calm. Lord, please show me where You are in the storm. (Write the ideas and words that come to mind for you.)

3) Holy Spirit, I know You are with me always. Please help me feel Your presence and know Your love in the midst of this tempest. Please describe the work You are doing in me through this current challenge. (Journal everything you hear in your thoughts.)

Review the thoughts God gave you above. Is there a common theme in the impressions you recorded? Perhaps you heard a word that especially warms your heart today? What Scripture comes to mind as you review your notes? Use the concordance of your Bible to look up a word that especially stood out to you or a word that you heard more than once in your thoughts. Scan the list of occurrences of that word cited in Scripture. When you see a verse in the concordance that has special meaning for you today, the

Holy Spirit is highlighting that verse for you. Turn to that passage of Scripture and read it. Write the verse here. Then, write all further insights and confirmations the Holy Spirit gives you as you read and ponder God's Word for you today.

Prayer:

Holy Spirit, thank You for speaking to my heart even now. I praise You in this storm, Lord. You are worthy of all my praise. I thank You for Your work in me as I learn to depend on You for all things, in good times and bad. Father, I confess my pride of independence and ask You to forgive my shortcomings. I submit my spirit to Yours and ask that You continue to mature me to be more like Jesus. I ask this in His name. Amen.

Pursuing the Heart of God - Book 2

Day 11 ♥♥ Refining Fire

Ask God:

Lord, I am thankful that "in all things You work for the good of those who love You and are called according to Your purpose" (see Romans 8:28). Lord, You allow the fire of our trials and afflictions, in order to test us and purify us. Your refining fire of adversity will remove the dross, skim off the waste in our lives, and purify us like silver and gold. When the dross has been removed, You, the Silversmith, can make something of our lives. You can use our vessel to complete the purpose You fashioned us for. Lord, thank You for Your wisdom in allowing us to suffer trials, to refine us and mature us in our faith. We learn to trust more completely in You as You accompany us in the fiery furnace and transform us according to Your will and plan. Lord, how do You explain this?

Listen to God - A Message from His Heart:

O child of Mine, it is good you understand a portion of My ways. There are times when I spare you from challenges and troubles, yet other times I do not. I allow you to endure trials, and I use them *for your good*: to strengthen you; to perfect your faith; and to purify you, removing the unnecessary waste from your life. *I refine you as silver and test you as gold.*

Do not fear the heat of the fire; fire is your friend. The furnace will be only hot enough to soften your will to the point where I can fashion you into a masterpiece, even more beautiful. I am with you in the fiery furnace. *When you walk through the fire, you will not be burned; the flames will not set you ablaze.* Take My hand; I will walk you through the fire *into a place of abundance.*

Count it all joy whenever you face trials of many kinds because you know that the testing of your faith produces perseverance. Let perseverance finish its work so that you may be mature and complete, not lacking anything. I will not allow you to be tested beyond what you can handle. I give you My Spirit to strengthen you in your weakness. *I will renew your strength; you will soar on wings like eagles; you will run and not grow weary, you will walk and not be faint.*

My beloved one, submit your will to Mine. Gladly enter the fire of refinement. Permit Me to mold you and make you according to My will. *I sanctify you Myself.* I desire that you continually allow Me to work in your life to make you more and more like Myself. This work will best be accomplished in the fire of refinement and the truth of My Word. I would not ask you to do something I have not done Myself. Lay down your life, and yield to Me. I know what is best for you, and I desire only that. I want you to know how much I love you, My friend.

Romans 8:28; Zechariah 13:9; Isaiah 43:2; James 1:2-4; Isaiah 40:31; John 17:19

Supporting Scripture:

And we know that in all things God works for the good of those who love Him, who have been called according to His purpose.—Romans 8:28

This third I will put into the fire; I will refine them like silver and test them like gold. They will call on My name and I will answer them; I will say, 'They are My people,' and they will say, 'The LORD is our God.'"—Zechariah 13:9

When you pass through the waters, I will be with you; and when you pass through the rivers, they will not sweep over you. When you walk through the fire, you will not be burned; the flames will not set you ablaze."—Isaiah 43:2

²Consider it pure joy, my brothers and sisters, whenever you face trials of many kinds, ³because you know that the testing of your faith produces perseverance. ⁴Let perseverance finish its work so that you may be mature and complete, not lacking anything.— James 1:2-4

But those who hope in the LORD will renew their strength. They will soar on wings like eagles; they will run and not grow weary, they will walk and not be faint.—Isaiah 40:31

For them I sanctify myself, that they too may be truly sanctified."—John 17:19

Prayer:

Father God, my Silversmith, I delight in You. Thank You for loving me so much that You are willing to allow the trials which will refine me the most. Thank You for walking me through the flames and not letting me perish. I am grateful for the gift of Your Spirit, Who strengthens me when I am weak. Do not let any of these trials go to waste, Lord. Use them all for my good. Teach me Your ways, Lord. May I be like putty in the Potter's hand. Please speak to me now and show me more of Your beautiful heart for me. In Jesus' name I pray. Amen.

Personal Reflections:

1) From the **Listen to God** section above, pick out a phrase or two that spoke directly to your heart today. Write the words here:

2) As you re-read and think about the words you wrote above, record any additional words or thoughts that come to your mind:

3) Which of the words or thoughts you recorded above might be from God? Underline or highlight them. Does any Scripture come to mind as you re-read what you've written above? If so, write the portion of Scripture that you recall:

4) Turn to the concordance of your Bible and look up one of the words you recalled from Scripture. Scan the verses cited under the word you have referenced in the concordance and record the references of one or two of the verses that the Holy Spirit illumines with special meaning for you today:

5) Turn to each of the references you recorded above. Read the verse and the surrounding passages. Do any additional words or phrases have special meaning for you today? Perhaps something you needed to hear? Wisdom for a problem you face? An answer to a question? A timely word for a difficult circumstance you currently navigate? If so, record the Scripture or words here:

6) What further question(s) do you have for God today? Write them here:

7) Seek God for answers to the question(s) you wrote above. Ask God one of the questions, and then, sit quietly and wait for His reply. Record the first thought that enters your mind. Write all the thoughts you have as you sit and listen to the Lord:

8) Chances are good that the thoughts you recorded as you sat quietly waiting for the Lord's response were indeed thoughts whispered to you by the Holy Spirit within you.

Re-read the thoughts above and ask God to confirm the thoughts that are from Him. Record any new inspirations you hear in your thoughts now:

Identify the Voice:

Re-read the responses you've written to the previous few questions. Run them through the tests below. In each test, the characteristic of God's voice is listed before the OR and the characteristic of Satan's voice is listed after it. Do those thoughts recorded in the section above:

a. Align with the character of God OR the ways of Satan?
b. Agree with the Word of God OR contradict it?
c. Produce the peace of God in your soul OR stir up strife?
d. Convict you OR condemn you?
e. Bring spiritual clarity OR confusion?
f. Offer the Lord's wisdom, instruction, comfort, and encouragement OR cause you to feel doubt, fear, worry, or shame?
g. Bring emotional healing OR cause additional emotional pain?

Using the above tests as your guide, draw a line through any thoughts in the previous section that might be from your enemy, the devil. Take a minute to rebuke Satan aloud. Do not believe his lies or buy in to his accusations or condemnations that you identify in your thoughts.

Going Deeper in Two-way Conversation with God:

1) Almighty God, help me understand Your wisdom in allowing me to experience trials. (Record everything you experience in your thoughts.)

2) Jesus, my Savior, please rescue me from the flames and teach me the lesson You want me to know. What is Your heart for me in this trial? (Write all the words and ideas that enter your mind.)

3) Holy Spirit, my Paraclete, stay with me in this present adversity. Make my spirit willing to endure this trial and my mind open to the lessons You want me to learn in it. Help me to see this challenge through Your eyes. What outcome do You desire for me? (Journal all His thoughts and your impressions.)

Review the thoughts God gave you above. Is there a common theme in the impressions you recorded? Perhaps you heard a word that especially warms your heart today? What Scripture comes to mind as you review your notes? Use the concordance of your Bible to look up a word that especially stood out to you or a word that you heard more than once in your thoughts. Scan the list of occurrences of that word cited in Scripture. When you see a verse in the concordance that has special meaning for you today, the Holy Spirit is highlighting that verse for you. Turn to that passage of Scripture and read it. Write the verse here. Then, write all further insights and confirmations the Holy Spirit gives you as you read and ponder God's Word for you today.

Prayer:

Holy Spirit, thank You for the trials and the fire that refines me. Please use these trials for my good: mature my faith and trust in You; sanctify my spirit; teach me Your ways and Your wisdom. I submit myself to You; please take my hand and walk me through my challenges. Lord, do not let the flames set me ablaze, but rescue me before I perish. Thank You for Your presence next to me in the furnace that burns so hot. Refine me with Your fire, so that I may set the world on fire for You! In the name of Jesus Christ, I pray. Amen.

Pursuing the Heart of God - Book 2

Day 12 ♥♥ I Am with You

Ask God:

Lord, I hear and know in my mind that You are with me. I read Your promises in Your Word. I can repeat these verses in my head; however, sometimes it just doesn't seem real. My heart does not always *feel* alive with Your presence. Lord, help me to know how to feel the joy of Your presence at all times. Lord, renew a right and unwavering spirit within me. Please allow me to experience the fullness of Your Spirit today.

Listen to God - A Message from His Heart:

My beloved one, I will say it again for you: I am alive, and I live in you. You may not always feel My presence, but I am here with you at all times. Listen to My voice; know and feel the joy of My presence. Seek Me first; spend time with Me in the morning. I will give you a good start to your day. You may hear a word of encouragement from Me, or an instruction, a blessing, or a command I want you to carry out. Let's connect daily; I wait patiently for you to seek Me, because I love you. *Blessed are you when you acclaim Me, when you walk in the light of My presence. Rejoice in My name all day long.* Speak to Me throughout your day.

So do not fear, for I am with you. I will take care of you. I protect you and keep you safe from harm. I provide for you and meet all your needs. I love you and desire to meet with you daily. You may call on Me any time of the day or night. I live in you, and I am available to you at all times. *Seek Me; call on Me; I am near.*

You are never alone when you are walking in relationship with Jesus. *He is the great Shepherd of the sheep.* He will *leave the ninety-nine in the open country in search of the one lost sheep.* And when He finds it, *He joyfully places it on His shoulders and brings it home.* Feeling lost? Stop your wandering, little sheep. Jesus knows exactly where you are. *His sheep listen to His voice:* "Come home, little lamb. Come home." Listen and obey. *Come near to Me, and I will come near to you. Remain in Me, and I will remain in you.* Love Me by obeying Me, and *We will make Our home with you.*

Of course, when you sin, we must deal with it as quickly as possible. When convicted by the Holy Spirit, confess your sin and turn from it. Disobedience stands in the way of a close relationship with Me. I do not remain anywhere close to sin, so it separates you from Me. Quickly get rid of any roadblock that stands in the way of a close relationship with Me. *Those whom I love, I rebuke and discipline. So be earnest and repent. Here I am! I stand at the door and knock. If anyone hears My voice and opens the door, I will come in and eat with that person, and they with Me.* Feast on My words; enjoy My presence. Let us break bread together. I am Nourishment for your soul. I bring refreshment to your days and life to your spirit. *I am with you wherever you go.* Bear witness to My goodness; share the message of My love and salvation.

*Psalm 89:15-16; Isaiah 41:10; Isaiah 55:6;
Luke 15:4-6; John 10:3; James 4:8; John 15:4;
John 14:23; Revelation 3:19-20; Joshua 1:9*

Supporting Scripture:

[15]Blessed are those who have learned to acclaim You, who walk in the light of Your presence, LORD. [16]They rejoice in Your name all day long; they celebrate Your righteousness.—Psalm 89:15-16

"So do not fear, for I am with you; do not be dismayed, for I am your God. I will strengthen you and help you; I will uphold you with my righteous right hand."—Isaiah 41:10

"Seek the LORD while He may be found; call on Him while He is near."—Isaiah 55:6

[4]"Suppose one of you has a hundred sheep and loses one of them. Doesn't he leave the ninety-nine in the open country and go after the lost sheep until he finds it? [5]And when he finds it, he joyfully puts it on his shoulders [6]and goes home."—Luke 15:4-6

"The gatekeeper opens the gate for Him, and the sheep listen to His voice. He calls His own sheep by name and leads them out."—John 10:3

Come near to God and He will come near to you…—James 4:8

"Remain in Me, as I also remain in you. No branch can bear fruit by itself; it must remain in the vine. Neither can you bear fruit unless you remain in Me."—John 15:4

Jesus replied, "Anyone who loves Me will obey My teaching. My Father will love them, and We will come to them and make Our home with them."—John 14:23

[19]"Those whom I love I rebuke and discipline. So be earnest and repent. [20]Here I am! I stand at the door and knock. If anyone hears My voice and opens the door, I will come in and eat with that person, and they with Me."—Revelation 3:19-20

"Have I not commanded you? Be strong and courageous. Do not be afraid; do not be discouraged, for the LORD your God will be with you wherever you go."—Joshua 1:9

Prayer:

Dear Father in Heaven, the secret to feeling Your presence is spending time in two-way conversation with You. I must know You to feel You with me. I can know You by spending time in

Your Word and speaking with You in prayer. Lord, You promise that I will seek You and find You when I seek You with all my heart (see Jeremiah 29:13). Lord, I will seek You while You may be found; I will call on You while You are near (see Isaiah 55:6). Lord, hear my cries and answer me. Share Your heart with me now, O Lord, as we sit together in the secret place, my innermost thoughts. In Jesus' name I pray. Amen.

Personal Reflections:

1) From the **Listen to God** section above, pick out a phrase or two that spoke directly to your heart today. Write the words here:

2) As you re-read and think about the words you wrote above, record any additional words or thoughts that come to your mind:

3) Which of the words or thoughts you recorded above might be from God? Underline or highlight them. Does any Scripture come to mind as you re-read what you've written above? If so, write the portion of Scripture that you recall:

4) Turn to the concordance of your Bible and look up one of the words you recalled from Scripture. Scan the verses cited under the word you have referenced in the concordance and record the references of one or two of the verses that the Holy Spirit illumines with special meaning for you today:

5) Turn to each of the references you recorded above. Read the verse and the surrounding passages. Do any additional words or phrases have special meaning for you today? Perhaps something you needed to hear? Wisdom for a problem you face? An answer to a question? A timely word for a difficult circumstance you currently navigate? If so, record the Scripture or words here:

6) What further question(s) do you have for God today? Write them here:

7) Seek God for answers to the question(s) you wrote above. Ask God one of the questions, and then, sit quietly and wait for His reply. Record the first thought that enters your mind. Write all the thoughts you have as you sit and listen to the Lord:

8) Chances are good that the thoughts you recorded as you sat quietly waiting for the Lord's response were indeed thoughts whispered to you by the Holy Spirit within you. Re-read the thoughts above and ask God to confirm the thoughts that are from Him. Record any new inspirations you hear in your thoughts now:

Identify the Voice:

Re-read the responses you've written to the previous few questions. Run them through the tests below. In each test, the characteristic of God's voice is listed before the OR and the characteristic of

Satan's voice is listed after it. Do those thoughts recorded in the section above:

    a. Align with the character of God OR the ways of Satan?
    b. Agree with the Word of God OR contradict it?
    c. Produce the peace of God in your soul OR stir up strife?
    d. Convict you OR condemn you?
    e. Bring spiritual clarity OR confusion?
    f. Offer the Lord's wisdom, instruction, comfort, and encouragement OR cause you to feel doubt, fear, worry, or shame?
    g. Bring emotional healing OR cause additional emotional pain?

Using the above tests as your guide, draw a line through any thoughts in the previous section that might be from your enemy, the devil. Take a minute to rebuke Satan aloud. Do not believe his lies or buy in to his accusations or condemnations that you identify in your thoughts.

Going Deeper in Two-way Conversation with God:

    1) Father God, it amazes me that You desire a close relationship with me. Will You describe what that looks like to You? (Record every word and thought He gives you now.)

2) Jesus, my Friend, will You share Your heart with me now? You are Immanuel, God with us. How do I feel Your presence? What shall I do? (Write His thoughts that pop into your head.)

3) Holy Spirit, I am drawing near to You now. Will you draw near to me? Please convict me of anything that stands in the way of my relationship with God. (List any sins or shortcomings that the Holy Spirit reveals to you now. Confess your sin, and ask the Lord's forgiveness.)

Review the thoughts God gave you above. Is there a common theme in the impressions you recorded? Perhaps you heard a word that especially warms your heart today? What Scripture comes to mind as you review your notes? Use the concordance of your Bible to look up a word that especially stood out to you or a word that you heard more than once in your thoughts. Scan the list of occurrences of that word cited in Scripture. When you see a verse

in the concordance that has special meaning for you today, the Holy Spirit is highlighting that verse for you. Turn to that passage of Scripture and read it. Write the verse here. Then, write all further insights and confirmations the Holy Spirit gives you as you read and ponder God's Word for you today.

Prayer:

Lord God Almighty, thank You for the work on the cross of Your Son, Jesus Christ, Who provided me the way back to You. Thank You that I may personally approach You any time. I am grateful that You want to enjoy a relationship with me, Your child. I do not deserve any amount of time You give Me, and yet You are generous to remain with me always. Thank You for sharing Your heart and what it means to be in relationship with You, and for Your forgiveness when I fall short. Lord, I love spending time with You. Holy Spirit, please help me to make it a regular practice, in good times and bad, every day, all day. In the name of Jesus, my Savior, I pray. Amen.

Pursuing the Heart of God - Book 2

Day 13 ♥♥ A Stay-In Order: Stay in Me

Ask God:

Lord, as I write this now during a pandemic, the state governor has issued a stay-in, stay-safe order. It keeps getting extended due to a daily increase in reported COVID-19 cases, hospitalizations, and deaths. Father, please comfort those who have lost a loved one to COVID-19. Provide for those who have lost their livelihood. Make Your presence and companionship known to those struggling with isolation. Lord, please help and sustain those who find themselves trying to balance work and the demands of remote schooling for children. All these difficulties drive us to be more dependent on You, to strengthen our relationship with You, to 'stay in' You.

Father, You are the only one Who can bring us through this challenging situation while maturing our faith. Lord, I will give You thanks in the middle of this difficulty, because it has given me more time to spend with You. And even when COVID-19 is controlled in the future, this circumstance has been a reminder of my dependence on You, as well as, Your desire that I spend more time with You and 'stay in' conversation with You. For that, I am grateful. What a huge gift it has been to rekindle the romance of an intimate relationship with You, my Bridegroom. Lord, what is on Your heart for me to learn and accomplish during this gift of extra time You have given me to spend with You?

Listen to God - A Message from His Heart:

My darling, My bride, My heart for you is to do exactly as you have been doing since this stay-in order was established: **Stay in Me**. What does that mean? Return to Me. Seek Me. Come near to Me. Remain in Me. Hope in Me. Trust in Me. Pray to Me. Believe in Me. Have faith in Me. Talk to Me. Ask Me. Tell Me. Listen to

Me. Know all of Me. Love Me. Obey Me. Acknowledge Me. Acclaim Me. Witness for Me. Share Me. Worship Me. Glorify Me.

Remain faithful to Me, for I am your Husband. *I betroth you to Me.* **Stay in** relationship with Me. Do not lust after other lovers. Do not put your trust in other gods. Do not turn to other pleasures instead of Me. Do not wander from the sheepfold. Do not get lost in obscurity. Do not become independent of Me, but be even more dependent on Me.

Stay in Me. I am the Lord, and I love you more than you will ever comprehend. I pray that you will be able *to grasp how wide and long and high and deep is the love of Christ for you, that you may know this love that surpasses knowledge and be filled to the measure of all the fullness of God.* You may be confident in Me and trust in Me because you know the greatness of My love for you.

I am your Bridegroom. Your greatest joy comes from knowing Me personally and intimately. Know Who I am. Know My ways. Know My promises. Know My Word. **Stay in** relationship with Me. Fear Me in awe and reverence, walk in obedience to Me, love Me, and *serve Me with all your heart and all your soul.* Put Me ahead of everything else in your life. I want to be first; *I am a jealous God.* I am protective of our time alone together and our relationship.

I desire to **stay in** daily communication with you. Meet Me in the secret place, your innermost thoughts, and pursue Me with all your heart. Speak to Me and listen to Me. *Call to Me, and I will answer you and tell you great and unsearchable things you do not know.* I want what is best for you. *No human mind has conceived what I have prepared for those who love Me. My plans are to prosper you and give you hope and a future. I will do immeasurably more than all you ask or imagine, according to My power that is at work within you.* I have given you My gift of the Holy Spirit Who **stays**

in you; please honor that gift by **staying in Me;** stay in and stay safe in Me. I care about you, My friend.

Hosea 2:19; Ephesians 3:18-19; Deuteronomy 10:12;
Deuteronomy 4:24; Jeremiah 33:3; 1 Corinthians 2:9;
Jeremiah 29:11; Ephesians 3:20

Supporting Scripture:

"I will betroth you to Me forever; I will betroth you in righteousness and justice, in love and compassion."—Hosea 2:19

[18]may have power, together with all the Lord's holy people, to grasp how wide and long and high and deep is the love of Christ, [19]and to know this love that surpasses knowledge—that you may be filled to the measure of all the fullness of God.—Ephesians 3:18-19

And now, Israel, what does the LORD your God ask of you but to fear the LORD your God, to walk in obedience to Him, to love Him, to serve the LORD your God with all your heart and with all your soul.—Deuteronomy 10:12

For the LORD your God is a consuming fire, a jealous God.—Deuteronomy 4:24

"Call to Me and I will answer you and tell you great and unsearchable things you do not know."—Jeremiah 33:3

However, as it is written: "What no eye has seen, what no ear has heard, and what no human mind has conceived"—the things God has prepared for those who love Him.—1 Corinthians 2:9

"For I know the plans I have for you," declares the LORD, "plans to prosper you and not to harm you, plans to give you hope and a future."—Jeremiah 29:11

Now to Him Who is able to do immeasurably more than all we ask or imagine, according to His power that is at work within us,— Ephesians 3:20

Prayer:

My faithful Bridegroom, I love You with all my heart. I will seek You in the morning and anticipate hearing Your voice. I, too, desire to communicate with You in a more intimate way. I cherish the time we spend together each morning, and I will be more diligent to remember to speak with You throughout the day. You are my Life Coach, my Daily Bread, my Living Water, my Champion, and my Friend. I will depend on You to meet all my needs. Spirit of God, please speak to me now in a more personal way, so that I know deeper places of Your heart. In the name of Jesus Christ, I pray. Amen.

Personal Reflections:

1) From the **Listen to God** section above, pick out a phrase or two that spoke directly to your heart today. Write the words here:

2) As you re-read and think about the words you wrote above, record any additional words or thoughts that come to your mind:

3) Which of the words or thoughts you recorded above might be from God? Underline or highlight them. Does any Scripture come to mind as you re-read what you've written above? If so, write the portion of Scripture that you recall:

4) Turn to the concordance of your Bible and look up one of the words you recalled from Scripture. Scan the verses cited under the word you have referenced in the concordance and record the references of one or two of the verses that the Holy Spirit illumines with special meaning for you today:

5) Turn to each of the references you recorded above. Read the verse and the surrounding passages. Do any additional words or phrases have special meaning for you today? Perhaps something you needed to hear? Wisdom for a problem you face? An answer to a question? A timely word for a difficult circumstance you currently navigate? If so, record the Scripture or words here:

6) What further question(s) do you have for God today? Write them here:

7) Seek God for answers to the question(s) you wrote above. Ask God one of the questions, and then, sit quietly and wait for His reply. Record the first thought that enters your mind. Write all the thoughts you have as you sit and listen to the Lord:

8) Chances are good that the thoughts you recorded as you sat quietly waiting for the Lord's response were indeed thoughts whispered to you by the Holy Spirit within you. Re-read the thoughts above and ask God to confirm the thoughts that are from Him. Record any new inspirations you hear in your thoughts now:

Identify the Voice:

Re-read the responses you've written to the previous few questions. Run them through the tests below. In each test, the characteristic of God's voice is listed before the OR and the characteristic of Satan's voice is listed after it. Do those thoughts recorded in the section above:

a. Align with the character of God OR the ways of Satan?
b. Agree with the Word of God OR contradict it?
c. Produce the peace of God in your soul OR stir up strife?
d. Convict you OR condemn you?
e. Bring spiritual clarity OR confusion?
f. Offer the Lord's wisdom, instruction, comfort, and encouragement OR cause you to feel doubt, fear, worry, or shame?
g. Bring emotional healing OR cause additional emotional pain?

Using the above tests as your guide, draw a line through any thoughts in the previous section that might be from your enemy, the devil. Take a minute to rebuke Satan aloud. Do not believe his lies or buy in to his accusations or condemnations that you identify in your thoughts.

Going Deeper in Two-way Conversation with God:

1) Father God, I will **stay in** You. Please show me the best way to accomplish that in my life and current situation. (Record every thought that enters your mind.)

2) Jesus Christ, please reveal Your heart for my relationship with You. What do You desire, and what does it look like for me? (Write down all words and ideas He gives you.)

3) Holy Spirit, thank You for **staying in** me; help me to **stay in** You. How do I walk in step with You and remain in constant communication with You? You know me the best. How is this best accomplished in my life? (Journal every impression, every thought, every idea the Holy Spirit prompts you with right now.)

Review the thoughts God gave you above. Is there a common theme in the impressions you recorded? Perhaps you heard a word that especially warms your heart today? What Scripture comes to mind as you review your notes? Use the concordance of your Bible to look up a word that especially stood out to you or a word that you heard more than once in your thoughts. Scan the list of occurrences of that word cited in Scripture. When you see a verse in the concordance that has special meaning for you today, the Holy Spirit is highlighting that verse for you. Turn to that passage of Scripture and read it. Write the verse here. Then, write all further insights and confirmations the Holy Spirit gives you as you read and ponder God's Word for you today.

Prayer:

Merciful Father, thank You for Your desire for a greater intimacy with me. It is difficult to comprehend the depth of Your love for me, Your child. I am in awe of Your character and Your ways. I am so blessed by You, and I pray I may be that kind of blessing to others on Your behalf. God, thank You for Your great love and grace. Holy Spirit, please **stay in** me and let me experience all the fullness of Your heart. Thank You for the abundant life in the Spirit. In the name of Jesus, my Lord, I pray. Amen.

Pursuing the Heart of God - Book 2

Day 14 ♥♥ Confess Your Sin

Ask God:

Lord, I confess I am sinful, and my sins separate me from You. Lord, I do not want to live a life apart from You. Please forgive my sins, and help me feel the conviction of Your Holy Spirit every time I fall short of Your glory. Father, may I be quick to respond and confess my sin. Holy Spirit, empower me to turn away from temptation and sin—to turn and walk away from it every time. Lord, sanctify me and make me more like Jesus. Teach me Your ways, and fashion me after Your will. Help me to pay attention to Your voice within me, to listen and obey.

Listen to God - A Message from His Heart:

O child of Mine, *you are not your own; you were bought with a price*—the death of My Son, Jesus Christ. Do not feel free to go your own way and continue in disobedience and rebellion. Partial obedience does not equal obedience. All sin, no matter how small, is disobedience. When you obey Me, I know that you love Me. I will not be anywhere near sin or those who sin. Do not let sin set you apart from Me, but remain in relationship with Me with your love and obedience.

All have sinned and fall short of My glory. But I loved you so much that *while you were still sinners, I sent My Son, Jesus Christ, to die for your sin*. Death is the required penalty for your sin, but My free *gift to you is eternal life*, when you believe in Me and confess your sin. *Confess with your mouth, "Jesus is Lord," and believe in your heart that I raised Him from the dead, and you will be saved.*

I love you so much that I gave My one and only Son, Jesus. Whoever believes in Him shall not die but experience eternal life.

He came to save you from a life of sin, disobedience, and rebellion. *When you confess your sin, I am faithful and just and will forgive you all your sin and purify you.*

Repent of your sin, turn and walk away from it. Do not continue in your sinful nature when you have the Spirit of God living in you. In Christ, you have crucified the flesh and no longer need to walk in it. *But since you now live according to the Spirit, stay in step with the Spirit of God.* Live in the freedom I provide. *You are a new creation in Jesus Christ; the old is gone, the new is here.* Live as the new person you are, claiming your victory in the shed blood of Jesus Christ for you.

When necessary, confess your sins to each other. Seek forgiveness when you have wronged another. You have been forgiven much; therefore, you will be required to forgive as much. Do not be generous with your judgment and stingy with your forgiveness, *but forgive one another as you also have been forgiven.*

1 Corinthians 6:19-20; Romans 3:23; Romans 5:8; Romans 6:23; Romans 10:9; John 3:16; 1 John 1:9; Galatian 5:25; 2 Corinthians 5:17; Colossians 3:13

Supporting Scripture:

[19]Do you not know that your bodies are temples of the Holy Spirit, Who is in you, Whom you have received from God? You are not your own; [20]you were bought with a price. Therefore honor God with your bodies.—1 Corinthians 6:19-20

For all have sinned and fall short of the glory of God.—Romans 3:23

But God demonstrates His own love for us in this: While we were still sinners, Christ died for us.—Romans 5:8

For the wages of sin is death, but the gift of God is eternal life in Christ Jesus our Lord.—Romans 6:23

If you declare with your mouth, "Jesus is Lord," and believe in your heart that God raised Him from the dead, you will be saved.—Romans 10:9

For God so loved the world that He gave His one and only Son, that whoever believes in Him shall not perish but have eternal life.—John 3:16

If we confess our sins, He is faithful and just and will forgive us our sins and purify us from all unrighteousness.—1 John 1:9

Since we live by the Spirit, let us keep in step with the Spirit.—Galatians 5:25

Therefore, if anyone is in Christ, the new creation has come: The old has gone, the new is here!—2 Corinthians 5:17

Bear with each other and forgive one another if any of you has a grievance against someone. Forgive as the Lord forgave you.—Colossians 3:13

Prayer:

Heavenly Father, thank You for providing Jesus Christ, the Way to be reconciled to you despite all my sin. Thank You for loving me even though I am sinful and for giving the gift of Your Son to die in my place. Lord, I am so grateful that I may experience Your grace and forgiveness when I confess my sins to You. Lord, please share Your heart with me in a more personal way right now. What do I need to change? What do You see in me? Please pour into my heart directly from Yours, as living water pouring into a lake. In the name of Jesus, I pray. Amen.

Personal Reflections:

1) From the **Listen to God** section above, pick out a phrase or two that spoke directly to your heart today. Write the words here:

2) As you re-read and think about the words you wrote above, record any additional words or thoughts that come to your mind:

3) Which of the words or thoughts you recorded above might be from God? Underline or highlight them. Does any Scripture come to mind as you re-read what you've written above? If so, write the portion of Scripture that you recall:

4) Turn to the concordance of your Bible and look up one of the words you recalled from Scripture. Scan the verses cited under the word you have referenced in the concordance and record the references of one or two of the verses that the Holy Spirit illumines with special meaning for you today:

.

5) Turn to each of the references you recorded above. Read the verse and the surrounding passages. Do any additional words or phrases have special meaning for you today? Perhaps something you needed to hear? Wisdom for a problem you face? An answer to a question? A timely word for a difficult circumstance you currently navigate? If so, record the Scripture or words here:

6) What further question(s) do you have for God today? Write them here:

7) Seek God for answers to the question(s) you wrote above. Ask God one of the questions, and then, sit quietly and wait for His reply. Record the first thought that enters your mind. Write all the thoughts you have as you sit and listen to the Lord:

8) Chances are good that the thoughts you recorded as you sat quietly waiting for the Lord's response were indeed thoughts whispered to you by the Holy Spirit within you. Re-read the thoughts above and ask God to confirm the thoughts that are from Him. Record any new inspirations you hear in your thoughts now:

Identify the Voice:

Re-read the responses you've written to the previous few questions. Run them through the tests below. In each test, the characteristic of God's voice is listed before the OR and the characteristic of Satan's voice is listed after it. Do those thoughts recorded in the section above:

   a. Align with the character of God OR the ways of Satan?
   b. Agree with the Word of God OR contradict it?
   c. Produce the peace of God in your soul OR stir up strife?
   d. Convict you OR condemn you?
   e. Bring spiritual clarity OR confusion?
   f. Offer the Lord's wisdom, instruction, comfort, and encouragement OR cause you to feel doubt, fear, worry, or shame?
   g. Bring emotional healing OR cause additional emotional pain?

Using the above tests as your guide, draw a line through any thoughts in the previous section that might be from your enemy, the devil. Take a minute to rebuke Satan aloud. Do not believe his lies or buy in to his accusations or condemnations that you identify in your thoughts.

Going Deeper in Two-way Conversation with God:

1) Father, please forgive me, for I have sinned. I confess my sin and weakness in this area:_____ (fill in the blank). I ask Your forgiveness in the name of Jesus by His blood. Lord, what do You want to share with me about this? (Record all that you hear.)

2) Jesus, my atoning, sacrificial Lamb of God, thank You for taking away my sin. Please tell me what You want me to know about Your love and Your sacrifice. (Write down every word and thought you receive.)

3) Holy Spirit, thank You for Your convicting work in my heart. Please reveal any other layers of sin that need to be confessed regarding this situation. Tell me what I need to do. (Journal everything you hear, think, and feel. Then be obedient to what He asks you to do.)

Review the thoughts God gave you above. Is there a common theme in the impressions you recorded? Perhaps you heard a word that especially warms your heart today? What Scripture comes to mind as you review your notes? Use the concordance of your Bible to look up a word that especially stood out to you or a word that you heard more than once in your thoughts. Scan the list of occurrences of that word cited in Scripture. When you see a verse in the concordance that has special meaning for you today, the Holy Spirit is highlighting that verse for you. Turn to that passage of Scripture and read it. Write the verse here. Then, write all further insights and confirmations the Holy Spirit gives you as you read and ponder God's Word for you today.

Prayer:

Father, Son, and Holy Spirit, I appreciate all that You have done for me. I thank You for working together to accomplish in me the work You have started in me. I am a work in progress, and I am grateful that You are patient with me every time I fail. Thank You for picking me back up, brushing me off, and setting my feet back on Your firm foundation. Thank You for second chances, and third, and fourth. I love You, and I will do better in the future with Your help. I cannot do any of this on my own. I am completely dependent on You, so I submit myself to You now. I commend my spirit into the hands of Your Spirit and ask that You will carry on Your continual redemptive renovation work in me. In the name of Jesus, my Redeemer, I pray. Amen.

Pursuing the Heart of God - Book 2

Day 15 ♥♥ Fully Forgiven

Ask God:

Father God in heaven, I have the head knowledge that I am forgiven. I have confessed my sin, invited Jesus into my heart to be my Savior and Lord, and know that He died for my sins, so that I could experience Your grace and forgiveness through a saving relationship in Christ. But so many times I have held on to past sins. I continue to ask forgiveness for the same sins when You have already forgiven me and forgotten them long ago. Lord, how do I completely rid myself of the shame, let go of the guilt, and release the claim to my sins? How do I know that I am fully forgiven? How might I be freed from this burden?

Listen to God - A Message from His Heart:

O child of Mine, you are being harder on yourself than I have been on you. Let Me release you from your burden of guilt and *set you free with the truth. When the Son sets you free, you will be free indeed.*

Your sin separated you from Me. There was nothing you could do to make that right. It is solely by My amazing grace and the death of My Son, Jesus Christ, on the cross that you may experience the forgiveness of sins and the hope of eternal life. Accepting Jesus as your Savior and believing that He died for your sin is the only way to be reconciled to Me.

When you invited Jesus into your heart to be your Savior, you were *crucified with Christ. You no longer live, but Christ lives in you.* When *your old self was crucified with Him,* your former body ruled by sin was *done away with,* so that you are *no longer a slave to sin*—you were set free. Let Me say it again: *When the Son sets you free, you are free indeed.* Believe it, and walk in the freedom I provide.

When I adopted you as My child, *I sent the Spirit of My Son, Jesus, into your heart. The Spirit calls out, "Abba Father." You are no longer a slave but My child; and since you are My child, I have made you My heir.* Not only are you fully forgiven; you are fully Mine. You belong to Me, and I love you. I am your loving Abba Father, your Daddy, and you are My sweet child.

You have My assurance that you are fully forgiven. It is up to you to fully believe it and fully accept My forgiveness—all of it. *I remember your sins no more*, and you would do well to accomplish this also. When you hold onto your sin, you are demonstrating a false belief that makes Jesus' work on the cross all in vain—saying that His death was not enough. But I tell you, it was. Do not discount the work of Christ on the cross. I gave Him up for you. Please accept that gift fully and fully believe it.

Do not allow the enemy to keep you in the prison cell of sin and guilt when you have been rescued and redeemed. *In Christ, you have redemption through His blood, the forgiveness of sins, in accordance with the riches of My grace.* Your sins were completely atoned for and I have *washed you whiter than snow.* I love you; I died for you; you are My child; and you are forgiven. Receive it and believe it in full.

John 8:32; John 8:36; Galatians 2:20;
Romans 6:6-7; Galatians 4:6-7;
Isaiah 43:25; Ephesians 1:7; Psalm 51:7

Supporting Scripture:

"Then you will know the truth, and the truth will set you free."— John 8:32

"So if the Son set you free, you will be free indeed."—John 8:36

I have been crucified with Christ and I no longer live, but Christ lives in me. The life I now live in the body, I live by faith in the Son of God, Who loved me and gave Himself for me.—Galatians 2:20

[6]For we know that our old self was crucified with Him so that the body ruled by sin might be done away with, that we should no longer be slaves to sin—[7]because anyone who has died has been set free from sin.—Romans 6:6-7

[6]Because you are His sons, God sent the Spirit of His Son into our hearts, the Spirit Who calls out, "*Abba*, Father." [7]So you are no longer a slave, but God's child; and since you are His child, God has made you also an heir.—Galatians 4:6-7

"I, even I, am He Who blots out your transgressions, for My own sake, and remembers your sins no more."—Isaiah 43:25

In Him we have redemption through His blood, the forgiveness of sins, in accordance with the riches of God's grace.—Ephesians 1:7

Cleanse me with hyssop, and I will be clean; wash me, and I will be whiter than snow.—Psalm 51:7

Prayer:

Abba Father, Daddy in heaven, thank You for Your gift of grace and forgiveness. I confess that I did not fully accept Your gift. Please forgive me. I believe it and receive it anew. I bind up Satan in the name of Jesus, by His shed blood. I claim victory over sin; I am free. I am a new person in Jesus Christ. I am no longer in bondage to sin; I am free and adopted by God as His child. Holy Spirit, please speak to me more personally right now, and share what's on Your heart. In the name of Jesus, my Savior, I pray. Amen.

Personal Reflections:

1) From the **Listen to God** section above, pick out a phrase or two that spoke directly to your heart today. Write the words here:

2) As you re-read and think about the words you wrote above, record any additional words or thoughts that come to your mind:

3) Which of the words or thoughts you recorded above might be from God? Underline or highlight them. Does any Scripture come to mind as you re-read what you've written above? If so, write the portion of Scripture that you recall:

4) Turn to the concordance of your Bible and look up one of the words you recalled from Scripture. Scan the verses cited under the word you have referenced in the concordance and

record the references of one or two of the verses that the Holy Spirit illumines with special meaning for you today:

5) Turn to each of the references you recorded above. Read the verse and the surrounding passages. Do any additional words or phrases have special meaning for you today? Perhaps something you needed to hear? Wisdom for a problem you face? An answer to a question? A timely word for a difficult circumstance you currently navigate? If so, record the Scripture or words here:

6) What further question(s) do you have for God today? Write them here:

7) Seek God for answers to the question(s) you wrote above. Ask God one of the questions, and then, sit quietly and wait for His reply. Record the first thought that enters your mind. Write all the thoughts you have as you sit and listen to the Lord:

8) Chances are good that the thoughts you recorded as you sat quietly waiting for the Lord's response were indeed thoughts whispered to you by the Holy Spirit within you. Re-read the thoughts above and ask God to confirm the thoughts that are from Him. Record any new inspirations you hear in your thoughts now:

Identify the Voice:

Re-read the responses you've written to the previous few questions. Run them through the tests below. In each test, the characteristic of God's voice is listed before the OR and the characteristic of Satan's voice is listed after it. Do those thoughts recorded in the section above:

a. Align with the character of God OR the ways of Satan?
b. Agree with the Word of God OR contradict it?
c. Produce the peace of God in your soul OR stir up strife?
d. Convict you OR condemn you?
e. Bring spiritual clarity OR confusion?
f. Offer the Lord's wisdom, instruction, comfort, and encouragement OR cause you to feel doubt, fear, worry, or shame?
g. Bring emotional healing OR cause additional emotional pain?

Using the above tests as your guide, draw a line through any thoughts in the previous section that might be from your enemy, the devil. Take a minute to rebuke Satan aloud. Do not believe his lies or buy in to his accusations or condemnations that you identify in your thoughts.

Going Deeper in Two-way Conversation with God:

1) Father God, tell me what it means to be Your child. (Write down everything you hear: words, phrases, verses, etc.)

2) Jesus, Lover of my soul, please help me understand more fully how I was crucified with You on the cross and how You set me free. (Record the ideas and thoughts He gives you now.)

3) Holy Spirit, empower me to discard the old false belief and fully embrace the truth. What do I need to do to accomplish this? (Journal everything you hear in your head.)

Review the thoughts God gave you above. Is there a common theme in the impressions you recorded? Perhaps you heard a word that especially warms your heart today? What Scripture comes to mind as you review your notes? Use the concordance of your Bible to look up a word that especially stood out to you or a word that you heard more than once in your thoughts. Scan the list of occurrences of that word cited in Scripture. When you see a verse in the concordance that has special meaning for you today, the Holy Spirit is highlighting that verse for you. Turn to that passage of Scripture and read it. Write the verse here. Then, write all further insights and confirmations the Holy Spirit gives you as you read and ponder God's Word for you today.

Prayer:

Dear Lord, thank You for helping me to better understand what forgiveness means. Thank You for remembering my sins no more; please help me to do the same. Help me fight against the devil when he accuses me of sins that have already been forgiven by You. Help me claim my identity as Your child and fully accept the forgiveness and the freedom that brings. In Jesus' name I pray. Amen.

Pursuing the Heart of God - Book 2

Day 16 ♥♥ God's Guidance

Ask God:

Lord, so many times, I run ahead of You and make my decisions without Your wisdom and guidance. Help Me to remember that You are always with me, watching over me, protecting me, and You have my best interests in mind. When I seek You, I will find You, and Your Spirit will make Your heart known to me. I submit myself to You and ask You to guide my ways. Strengthen me to carry out all that You created me for; to fulfill the purpose You had in mind for me since before You created the world. Please guide me down that path and empower me to further Your kingdom.

Listen to God - A Message from His Heart:

My sons and daughters, I am never too busy to listen to you. I am available to you all hours of the day and night. *I never slumber nor sleep.* You need My wisdom. *If you lack wisdom, ask Me. I give generously to all without finding fault. But when you ask, you must believe and not doubt. Ask and it will be given to you.* I know what you need, but I want you to ask.

Whatever situation you face, I have the answer. I will teach you from My Word. *My Word is a lamp for your feet, a light on your path.* Meditate, or thoughtfully ponder, on my Word day and night, and it will become clearer to you. My Spirit helps you understand My Word. I will instruct you with the truth and in My perfect timing. I will lead you on the path I have prepared for you and designated for you. I will keep you in My sight at all times. My lovingkindness will surround you; I will protect you on every side. You will experience My peace and joy, even in your biggest trials.

I have plans to prosper you and not to harm you, plans to give you hope and a future. Call on Me and I will listen to you. Seek Me and find Me when you seek Me with all your heart. Sit with Me and seek My heart. I hear your requests. *When you ask for anything according to My will, have faith and believe I will give you what you asked for.*

I know the future, and I know what's best for you. *My Spirit will guide you into all truth and tell you what is yet to come.* He will help you discern between truth and falsehoods. He will equip you for the plans I have made for you. He will empower you to carry out the purpose for which I created you. He will warn you of dangers that lie ahead. He will encourage you to live in a manner that will bring glory to Me. Pay attention to My Spirit within, and your ears will *hear My voice saying, "This is the way; walk in it."*

I reveal things to you by My Spirit; He knows the deep things of My heart and freely gives them to you. Blessed are you when you *wait for Me*! Even when you do not know what to ask for, the *Spirit intercedes for you according to My will.*

Come to Me and listen to Me. *I will instruct you and teach you in the way you should go; I will counsel you with My loving eye on you.* Trust in Me alone. When you do not follow My instructions, there will be consequences. Do not be too hasty to make your own decisions and walk in your own way. In the end, *your pride* will reap you a harvest of *destruction.* Every decision you make is an important one, big or small. Involve Me in each one.

Trust in Me with all your heart, and lean not on your own understanding; in all your ways submit to Me, and I will make your paths straight. Do not run ahead and try to fix things on your own. You'll most assuredly be disappointed in the end. Exercise forbearance and *wait for Me. I will act on your behalf.* When you walk down the path I place you on, your obedience will lead to blessings. Your best blessings are the result of listening to My voice and following My instructions. You are never alone. I am with you always. Why try to do things on your own? *Listen to My voice and follow Me.*

Psalm 121:3-4; James 1:5-6; Psalm 119:105;
Jeremiah 29:11-13; Mark 11:24; John 16:13; Isaiah 30:21;
1 Corinthians 2:10; Isaiah 30:18; Romans 8:26; Psalm 32:8;
Proverbs 16:18; Proverbs 3:5-6; Isaiah 64:4; John 10:27

Supporting Scripture:

[3]He will not let your foot slip—He Who watches over you will not slumber; [4]indeed, He Who watches over Israel will neither slumber nor sleep.—Psalm 121:3-4

[5]If any of you lacks wisdom, you should ask God, Who gives generously to all without finding fault, and it will be given to you. [6]But when you ask, you must believe and not doubt, because the one who doubts is like a wave of the sea, blown and tossed by the wind.—James 1:5-6

Your word is a lamp for my feet, a light on my path.—Psalm 119:105

[11]"For I know the plans I have for you," declares the LORD, "plans to prosper you and not to harm you, plans to give you hope and a future. [12]Then you will call on Me and come and pray to Me, and I will listen to you. [13]You will seek Me and find Me when you seek Me with all your heart."—Jeremiah 29:11-13

"Therefore I tell you, whatever you ask for in prayer, believe that you have received it, and it will be yours."—Mark 11:24

"But when He, the Spirit of truth, comes, He will guide you into all the truth. He will not speak on His own; He will speak only what He hears, and He will tell you what is yet to come."
—John 16:13

Whether you turn to the right or to the left, your ears will hear a voice behind you, saying, "This is the way; walk in it."—Isaiah 30:21

These are the things God has revealed to us by His Spirit. The Spirit searches all things, even the deep things of God.—1 Corinthians 2:10

Yet the LORD longs to be gracious to you; therefore He will rise up to show you compassion. For the LORD is a God of justice. Blessed are all who wait for Him!—Isaiah 30:18

In the same way, the Spirit helps us in our weakness. We do not know what we ought to pray for, but the Spirit Himself intercedes for us through wordless groans.—Romans 8:26

I will instruct you and teach you in the way you should go; I will counsel you with My loving eye on you.—Psalm 32:8

Pride goes before destruction, a haughty spirit before a fall.— Proverbs 16:18

5Trust in the LORD with all your heart, and lean not on your own understanding; 6in all your ways submit to Him and He will make your paths straight.—Proverbs 3:5-6

Since ancient times no one has heard, no ear has perceived, no eye has seen any God besides You, Who acts on behalf of those who wait for Him.—Isaiah 64:4

"My sheep listen to My voice; I know them, and they follow Me."—John 10:27

Prayer:

Lord, I am so blessed by Your Spirit within me Who teaches me all things, even the deep things of Your heart. I am so looking forward to hearing more of Your heart for me today. Holy Spirit, please speak to me as I seek You wholeheartedly today. I want to do Your will. I desire to know Your plans for me. Lord, please let me in on the next step in the race You designed for me and me for. In Jesus' name I pray. Amen.

Personal Reflections:

1) From the **Listen to God** section above, pick out a phrase or two that spoke directly to your heart today. Write the words here:

2) As you re-read and think about the words you wrote above, record any additional words or thoughts that come to your mind:

3) Which of the words or thoughts you recorded above might be from God? Underline or highlight them. Does any

Scripture come to mind as you re-read what you've written above? If so, write the portion of Scripture that you recall:

4) Turn to the concordance of your Bible and look up one of the words you recalled from Scripture. Scan the verses cited under the word you have referenced in the concordance and record the references of one or two of the verses that the Holy Spirit illumines with special meaning for you today:

5) Turn to each of the references you recorded above. Read the verse and the surrounding passages. Do any additional words or phrases have special meaning for you today? Perhaps something you needed to hear? Wisdom for a problem you face? An answer to a question? A timely word for a difficult circumstance you currently navigate? If so, record the Scripture or words here:

6) What further question(s) do you have for God today? Write them here:

7) Seek God for answers to the question(s) you wrote above. Ask God one of the questions, and then, sit quietly and wait for His reply. Record the first thought that enters your mind. Write all the thoughts you have as you sit and listen to the Lord:

8) Chances are good that the thoughts you recorded as you sat quietly waiting for the Lord's response were indeed thoughts whispered to you by the Holy Spirit within you. Re-read the thoughts above and ask God to confirm the thoughts that are from Him. Record any new inspirations you hear in your thoughts now:

Identify the Voice:

Re-read the responses you've written to the previous few questions. Run them through the tests below. In each test, the characteristic of God's voice is listed before the OR and the characteristic of Satan's voice is listed after it. Do those thoughts recorded in the section above:

a. Align with the character of God OR the ways of Satan?
b. Agree with the Word of God OR contradict it?
c. Produce the peace of God in your soul OR stir up strife?
d. Convict you OR condemn you?
e. Bring spiritual clarity OR confusion?
f. Offer the Lord's wisdom, instruction, comfort, and encouragement OR cause you to feel doubt, fear, worry, or shame?
g. Bring emotional healing OR cause additional emotional pain?

Using the above tests as your guide, draw a line through any thoughts in the previous section that might be from your enemy, the devil. Take a minute to rebuke Satan aloud. Do not believe his lies or buy in to his accusations or condemnations that you identify in your thoughts.

Going Deeper in Two-way Conversation with God:

1) Father God, I know You want the best for me. Lord, please show me what that means for me personally in my current challenge of _____ (fill in the blank). (Write down all thoughts and impressions you have in this moment.)

2) Jesus, You are the Way-maker. Please show me the way to Your heart. What must I do to get on the path to a deeper relationship with You? (Record everything you hear.)

3) Holy Spirit, You are my Helper and my Counselor. Please counsel me with the wisdom of God and help me know which way I should turn in my current dilemma or decision: _____ (fill in the blank). (Listen to His voice in your thoughts, and journal whatever pops into your mind.)

Review the thoughts God gave you above. Is there a common theme in the impressions you recorded? Perhaps you heard a word that especially warms your heart today? What Scripture comes to mind as you review your notes? Use the concordance of your Bible to look up a word that especially stood out to you or a word that you heard more than once in your thoughts. Scan the list of occurrences of that word cited in Scripture. When you see a verse in the concordance that has special meaning for you today, the Holy Spirit is highlighting that verse for you. Turn to that passage of Scripture and read it. Write the verse here. Then, write all further insights and confirmations the Holy Spirit gives you as you read and ponder God's Word for you today.

Prayer:

Most Holy One, I stand in awe that I can approach Your throne of grace any time of the day or night. Thank You for being available to me 24/7/365. I desire to know Your wisdom and Your will in all circumstances. Lord, Your eyes are forever on me; You know my coming and my going. Holy Spirit, I submit my spirit to Your leading. Please direct my paths and help me discern God's will and His ways. I will meditate on Your Word and receive my instruction from You. Holy Spirit, bring understanding as I read it. Point me to the Scripture You want me to know and cherish in my heart for today. In the name of Jesus Christ, my Lord. Amen.

Pursuing the Heart of God - Book 2

Day 17 ♥♥ Listen to God

Ask God:

Hello, Lord, are You there? I know that Your Holy Spirit is with me at all times because He lives in my heart, and You speak to me through Him. Do You speak to me often? Sometimes I try to be still and listen to You, but I cannot hear Your voice in my thoughts. I don't really know what it sounds like, or I'm not sure whether it's Your thoughts or mine. How do I know the difference? Holy Spirit, please help me be still enough to listen, and give me the discernment to know Your voice when You speak to me.

Listen to God - A Message from His Heart:

My beloved one, I am always right here waiting to listen to you and talk to you. Will you do the same for Me? I desire intimate relationship and personal conversation with you daily. I want to listen to your requests and impart My wisdom and instructions for your life. I am your Shepherd, and you are My sheep. *My sheep know My voice and follow Me.*

You will know and recognize My voice by spending time with Me in My Word. Whenever you read My Word, you are hearing directly from Me. The Holy Spirit will open your eyes to see what I want you to understand when you spend time in the Scripture. You will hear Me speak to you through My Word. However, I love to communicate with you in prayer also. When you pray, go into the secret place, your innermost thoughts, where you and I meet alone. *Be still and know that I am God.* When you quiet your heart and mind enough and give Me your undivided attention, you will hear My inaudible voice in your thoughts. It is soft as a whisper yet *powerful and majestic.*

When you spend time in My Word, getting to know My character better, you will better know what to expect when you hear Me in your thoughts. I am loving and compassionate; I will encourage you with My love and envelop you with My kindness. I am wise and discerning; I will *instruct you* with My wisdom. I am your *Advocate*; I will *teach you*, guide you, and support you with My knowledge. I am your *Counselor*; I will advise you in all your circumstances. I am your *Father*; I will delight in you and bestow your identity as My child. I am the *Prince of Peace*; I will fill you with the confidence and peace of knowing I am in control.

When you hear My voice, the message will always align with My Word in Scripture. My voice will always be consistent with My character. It will bring you a feeling of peace, unless I am convicting you of a sin. My words will never be harsh, accusing, condemning, or confusing like Satan's voice. My words in your thoughts will be sincere, clear, truthful, motivating, comforting, and uplifting. I may instruct you to do something challenging, but I will always equip you to carry it out. I will never ask you to do anything that does not agree with My Word in the Bible. I will not lie to you, manipulate you, deceive you, or shame you. Those actions identify your enemy, the devil. The more time you spend in conversation with Me, the better you will be able to identify and discern My voice from your own thoughts and Satan's.

Above all, I just want to spend time with you, however that works best: in My Word, in personal conversation, or shoulder to shoulder walking through the journey of your life. I love you, My friend, and I want what is best for you. It is best that you remain in relationship with Me by reading My Word, talking to Me in prayer, listening to Me and hearing My voice, loving Me with your obedience, and praising Me whenever possible. I look forward to our next conversation. When shall we meet again?

John 10:4; Psalm 46:10; Psalm 29:4;
Psalm 32:8; John 14:26; Isaiah 9:6

Supporting Scripture:

"When He has brought out all His own, He goes on ahead of them, and His sheep follow Him because they know His voice."—John 10:4

He says, "Be still, and know that I am God; I will be exalted among the nations, I will be exalted in the earth."—Psalm 46:10

The voice of the LORD is powerful; the voice of the LORD is majestic.—Psalm 29:4

"I will instruct you and teach you in the way you should go; I will counsel you with My loving eye on you."—Psalm 32:8

"But the Advocate, the Holy Spirit, Whom the Father will send in My name, will teach you all things and will remind you of everything I have said to you."—John 14:26

For to us a child is born, to us a Son is given, and the government will be on His shoulders. And He will be called Wonderful Counselor, Mighty God, Everlasting Father, Prince of Peace.—Isaiah 9:6

Prayer:

Heavenly Father, I so long to hear You speak more regularly and to know for sure it's Your voice I hear. Teach me more about Your character so that I may be confident in discerning Your voice from the other thoughts in my head. Holy Spirit, please speak to me now and let me know what needs to change in my life in order for me to hear Your voice in my thoughts more consistently. In Jesus' name I pray. Amen.

Personal Reflections:

1) From the **Listen to God** section above, pick out a phrase or two that spoke directly to your heart today. Write the words here:

2) As you re-read and think about the words you wrote above, record any additional words or thoughts that come to your mind:

3) Which of the words or thoughts you recorded above might be from God? Underline or highlight them. Does any Scripture come to mind as you re-read what you've written above? If so, write the portion of Scripture that you recall:

4) Turn to the concordance of your Bible and look up one of the words you recalled from Scripture. Scan the verses cited under the word you have referenced in the concordance and

record the references of one or two of the verses that the Holy Spirit illumines with special meaning for you today:

5) Turn to each of the references you recorded above. Read the verse and the surrounding passages. Do any additional words or phrases have special meaning for you today? Perhaps something you needed to hear? Wisdom for a problem you face? An answer to a question? A timely word for a difficult circumstance you currently navigate? If so, record the Scripture or words here:

6) What further question(s) do you have for God today? Write them here:

7) Seek God for answers to the question(s) you wrote above. Ask God one of the questions, and then, sit quietly and wait for His reply. Record the first thought that enters your

mind. Write all the thoughts you have as you sit and listen to the Lord:

8) Chances are good that the thoughts you recorded as you sat quietly waiting for the Lord's response were indeed thoughts whispered to you by the Holy Spirit within you. Re-read the thoughts above and ask God to confirm the thoughts that are from Him. Record any new inspirations you hear in your thoughts now:

Identify the Voice:

Re-read the responses you've written to the previous few questions. Run them through the tests below. In each test, the characteristic of God's voice is listed before the OR and the characteristic of Satan's voice is listed after it. Do those thoughts recorded in the section above:

    a. Align with the character of God OR the ways of Satan?
    b. Agree with the Word of God OR contradict it?
    c. Produce the peace of God in your soul OR stir up strife?

d. Convict you OR condemn you?
e. Bring spiritual clarity OR confusion?
f. Offer the Lord's wisdom, instruction, comfort, and encouragement OR cause you to feel doubt, fear, worry, or shame?
g. Bring emotional healing OR cause additional emotional pain?

Using the above tests as your guide, draw a line through any thoughts in the previous section that might be from your enemy, the devil. Take a minute to rebuke Satan aloud. Do not believe his lies or buy in to his accusations or condemnations that you identify in your thoughts.

Going Deeper in Two-way Conversation with God:

1) Father God, help me to quiet my mind and heart enough to hear You speak. What do You want me to know at this time? (Record every word or thought you have.)

2) Jesus, my Friend, will You share what You want me to know about listening to Your voice? How do I discern between Your voice and my own thoughts? (Write down what He says to you now.)

3) Holy Spirit, teach me to be more in tune with Your whispers and how You speak to me all day long. What do I need to do to hear You speaking to me and guiding me? (Journal all ideas and thoughts that pop into your mind.)

Review the thoughts God gave you above. Is there a common theme in the impressions you recorded? Perhaps you heard a word that especially warms your heart today? What Scripture comes to mind as you review your notes? Use the concordance of your Bible to look up a word that especially stood out to you or a word that you heard more than once in your thoughts. Scan the list of occurrences of that word cited in Scripture. When you see a verse in the concordance that has special meaning for you today, the Holy Spirit is highlighting that verse for you. Turn to that passage of Scripture and read it. Write the verse here. Then, write all further insights and confirmations the Holy Spirit gives you as you read and ponder God's Word for you today.

Prayer:

Dear Lord, thank You for speaking Your heart and pouring Your thoughts into my mind whenever I meet with You. Thank You for making Yourself available to meet with me anytime and anywhere. Lord, I so appreciate that Your desire is for greater intimacy with me. Give me the same desire and expand my time, so that I may accomplish the goal of putting You first in my life and listening to You daily. Thank You for Your lovingkindness and forbearance. In the name of Jesus Christ, I pray. Amen.

Pursuing the Heart of God - Book 2

Day 18 ♥♥ Where Is God?

Ask God:

Father, sometimes when painful things happen to us, we wonder where You are and why You would allow us to go through our trials, troubles, and challenges. Lord, will you speak to that question for me? Where are You in the midst of my toil, pain, and heartache?

Listen to God - A Message from His Heart:

My child, I am right there with you in the middle of your hardships and your pain. *In all your distress, I too am distressed.* I understand what you are going through; I Myself have experienced an even greater measure of emotional and physical pain and suffering. Where am I in your suffering? I am where the pain is. *I was crushed for your iniquities; the punishment that brought you peace was on Me.* You have My promise that in your challenges and in your suffering, *I will never leave you nor forsake you.*

Beloved one, I know your pain. I know your anger, your anxiety, your frustration, your hurt. *Cast all your anxiety on Me.* Give over your burdens, and exchange them for a lighter load. *Take My yoke upon you. My yoke is easy and My burden is light.* I will carry you through your difficulties. *Remain in Me and I will remain in you.* Find your peace in knowing that you are following My will and plans. You are doing the right thing. I know you do not understand My ways, but *in all things I will work for the good of those who love Me and are called according to My purpose.* You have been called by Me. You do not need to understand it all right now. I am always working behind the scenes to bring about My will, to bring about change in people who are willing to seek Me with their whole heart.

In your trials I carry you. As you were crucified with Me, you now must *take up your cross daily.* To follow Me, you must deny yourself. *You will seek Me and find Me when you seek Me with all your heart.* Seek Me in Your affliction, and you will find Me there. I do not leave you to walk through your valleys alone. I take you by the hand and guide you through the rough terrain and over the mountain peaks. I remove the obstacles that stand in your way. But I do not necessarily remove you from your troubles or remove your troubles from you. The lessons learned in affliction are often the most valuable teachings that mature your faith to a level that a life of all pleasure would never attain.

Submit yourself to Me. *Delight in Me, and I will give you the desires of your heart. I will prosper you, give you hope and a future.* The blessings from your obedience will be passed down from generation to generation of those who love Me. Hang in there. Do not be overwhelmed by the magnitude of this trial. I will carry you through. I will walk you through this challenge. There is a mountain of peace and blessing on the other side of this valley. Hold to the truth, and *the truth will set you free.*

I am setting you free from this emotional, physical, and financial burden. I will bless you seven times the cost of this trial. Your reward is from Me. Run for the prize. Do not look back. Do not look side to side in comparison with your brother or sister. Do not let the enemy overtake you and *cut in on you* or interrupt the race you are running with Me. I am your Running Mate. Together we will win this race and celebrate the joy of the rewards.

I love you, My child. Keep your head up, your eyes to the sky, and focus on Me, not your troubles. I am here. *I will never leave you* or forget about you. I will carry you through. You are My friend, My beloved child, the heir of everything that belongs to Me.

Isaiah 63:9; Isaiah 53:5; Joshua 1:5; 1 Peter 5:7; Matthew 11:29-30; John 15:4; Romans 8:28; Luke 9:23; Jeremiah 29:13; Psalm 37:4; Jeremiah 29:11; John 8:32; Galatians 5:7; Joshua 1:5

Supporting Scripture:

In all their distress He too was distressed, and the angel of His presence saved them. In His love and mercy He redeemed them; He lifted them up and carried them all the days of old.—Isaiah 63:9

But He was pierced for our transgressions, He was crushed for our iniquities; the punishment that brought us peace was on Him, and by His wounds we are healed.—Isaiah 53:5

"No one will be able to stand against you all the days of your life. As I was with Moses, so I will be with you; I will never leave you nor forsake you."—Joshua 1:5

Cast all your anxiety on Him because He cares for you.—1 Peter 5:7

[29]"Take My yoke upon you and learn from Me, for I am gentle and humble in heart, and you will find rest for your souls. [30]For My yoke is easy and My burden is light."—Matthew 11:29-30

"Remain in Me, as I also remain in you. No branch can bear fruit by itself; it must remain in the vine. Neither can you bear fruit unless you remain in Me."—John 15:4

And we know that in all things God works for the good of those who love Him, who have been called according to His purpose.—Romans 8:28

Then He said to them all: "Whoever wants to be My disciple must deny themselves and take up their cross daily and follow Me."—Luke 9:23

"You will seek Me and find Me when you seek Me with all your heart."—Jeremiah 29:13

Take delight in the LORD, and He will give you the desires of your heart.—Psalm 37:4

"For I know the plans I have for you," declares the LORD, "plans to prosper you and not to harm you, plans to give you hope and a future."—Jeremiah 29:11

"Then you will know the truth, and the truth will set you free."— John 8:32

You were running a good race. Who cut in on you to keep you from obeying the truth?—Galatians 5:7

"No one will be able to stand against you all the days of your life. As I was with Moses, so I will be with you; I will never leave you nor forsake you."—Joshua 1:5

Prayer:

Most Holy One, I thank You for Your love and kindness. I am grateful that I am never alone when I remain in relationship with You. Thank You for Your presence in my trials, even when I don't know it or feel it. I thank You for working in the background to cause the good to come out of every trial I face. Lord, I am secure in the confidence I have that You are in control and You want the best for me. I submit myself to You and ask that You share Your heart with me now about the challenges I am walking through today. Holy Spirit, please help me see Your hand in my life and know Your presence in every situation. In the name of Jesus, my Rescuer, I pray. Amen.

Personal Reflections:

1) From the **Listen to God** section above, pick out a phrase or two that spoke directly to your heart today. Write the words here:

2) As you re-read and think about the words you wrote above, record any additional words or thoughts that come to your mind:

3) Which of the words or thoughts you recorded above might be from God? Underline or highlight them. Does any Scripture come to mind as you re-read what you've written above? If so, write the portion of Scripture that you recall:

4) Turn to the concordance of your Bible and look up one of the words you recalled from Scripture. Scan the verses cited under the word you have referenced in the concordance and record the references of one or two of the verses that the Holy Spirit illumines with special meaning for you today:

5) Turn to each of the references you recorded above. Read the verse and the surrounding passages. Do any additional words or phrases have special meaning for you today? Perhaps something you needed to hear? Wisdom for a problem you face? An answer to a question? A timely word for a difficult circumstance you currently navigate? If so, record the Scripture or words here:

6) What further question(s) do you have for God today? Write them here:

7) Seek God for answers to the question(s) you wrote above. Ask God one of the questions, and then, sit quietly and wait for His reply. Record the first thought that enters your mind. Write all the thoughts you have as you sit and listen to the Lord:

8) Chances are good that the thoughts you recorded as you sat quietly waiting for the Lord's response were indeed

thoughts whispered to you by the Holy Spirit within you. Re-read the thoughts above and ask God to confirm the thoughts that are from Him. Record any new inspirations you hear in your thoughts now:

Identify the Voice:

Re-read the responses you've written to the previous few questions. Run them through the tests below. In each test, the characteristic of God's voice is listed before the OR and the characteristic of Satan's voice is listed after it. Do those thoughts recorded in the section above:

a. Align with the character of God OR the ways of Satan?
b. Agree with the Word of God OR contradict it?
c. Produce the peace of God in your soul OR stir up strife?
d. Convict you OR condemn you?
e. Bring spiritual clarity OR confusion?
f. Offer the Lord's wisdom, instruction, comfort, and encouragement OR cause you to feel doubt, fear, worry, or shame?
g. Bring emotional healing OR cause additional emotional pain?

Using the above tests as your guide, draw a line through any thoughts in the previous section that might be from your enemy, the devil. Take a minute to rebuke Satan aloud. Do not believe his lies or buy in to his accusations or condemnations that you identify in your thoughts.

Going Deeper in Two-way Conversation with God:

1) Father God, in the challenges I face today, what do You want me to learn from this experience? (Record every thought He gives you.)

2) Jesus, my Friend, please show me Your presence and compassion in my pain. Share Your heart for my suffering. (Write down all words and thoughts you hear.)

3) Holy Spirit, my Comforter, please ease my cares and share God's heart for me in this struggle. Why do I need to endure this pain? (Journal what He says to you.)

Review the thoughts God gave you above. Is there a common theme in the impressions you recorded? Perhaps you heard a word that especially warms your heart today? What Scripture comes to mind as you review your notes? Use the concordance of your Bible to look up a word that especially stood out to you or a word that you heard more than once in your thoughts. Scan the list of occurrences of that word cited in Scripture. When you see a verse in the concordance that has special meaning for you today, the Holy Spirit is highlighting that verse for you. Turn to that passage of Scripture and read it. Write the verse here. Then, write all further insights and confirmations the Holy Spirit gives you as you read and ponder God's Word for you today.

Prayer:

Dear Lord, thank You for being present with me at all times, through every challenge I face, guiding me through the valleys and climbing the mountains with me. I am so grateful for Your love and care. Holy Spirit, thank You for sharing Your heart with me now, and please give me a teachable heart to know and learn more about You and how You take care of me. In Jesus' name I pray. Amen.

Pursuing the Heart of God - Book 2

Day 19 ♥♥ A Person After My Own Heart

Ask God:

Lord, what does it mean to become a person after Your own heart? Please describe what that looks like. Help me see that person through Your eyes, and then teach me how to become that person and pursue You more passionately. Please instill in my heart Your passions and desires. O Lord, I will delight in You and discover more and more about You.

Listen to God - A Message from His Heart:

Sweet child of Mine, I created you for My enjoyment. I desire to have a deeply intimate relationship with you. I want to be involved in all aspects of your life. It pleases Me when you are eager to meet with Me in the secret place of your innermost thoughts, quieting your heart and mind enough to wait upon My voice. I speak to you often, whether you hear Me or not. Many times you do not discern My voice from your own thoughts because you do not anticipate that I will speak to you. The first step to hearing My voice is to expect and believe.

Here I am! I stand at the door and knock. If you hear My voice and open the door, I will come in and eat with you and you with Me. We will enjoy sweet communion and fellowship together. I hear all of your prayers and requests, but I ask that you leave room in the conversation for Me to speak also. I desire to encourage you, uplift you, teach you, guide you, comfort you, give you My wisdom, and pour out My love on you. You may experience all of Me when you put Me first and meet with Me daily, away from the noise and distractions.

Mary, the sister of Martha and Lazarus, was a woman who pursued My heart. She knew how to honor and please Me by *sitting at My feet, listening to what I said.* She eagerly waited in anticipation to hear every word that fell from My lips. She did not want to miss one thing I said. She endured the chastisement of her distracted sister, Martha, who was busy with all the preparations. Martha scolded Me to tell Mary to help her, but I would not. *Mary had chosen what was better, and I would not take that from her.* Mary wanted to hear everything I had to say and remained close to Me in order to hear Me. The way to experience a close relationship with Me is to sit with Me daily and eagerly listen to every word I speak.

Do not merely listen to My voice, but also obey it. *Anyone who loves Me will obey My teaching. My Father will love them, and We will come to them and make Our home with them. Love Me with all your heart, soul, and mind.* Demonstrate the fullness of your love by listening to Me and obeying Me in the things I teach you. You are My child, even My heir. Everything I have is yours. *Ask anything according to My will, and you will have what you asked of Me.*

My Spirit lives in you and empowers you *to grasp how wide and long and high and deep is the love of Christ and to know this love that surpasses knowledge—that you may be filled to the measure of all the fullness of God.* Let Me fill you to overflowing with My love, beyond your imagination. Know and feel My presence as you sit with Me in two-way conversation.

Will you meet with Me more often? Will you sit at My feet, listening to what I say? Do you desire to know what's on My heart? Will you spend more time in My Word getting to know Me better, so that you can believe My promises and discern My voice? Will you pursue Me as passionately as I have been pursuing you? I created you to love you, My child. *I know your inmost being*, and I desire that you would know Mine—what makes My heart come alive. Actively chase after Me and become a person *after My own heart.*

Revelation 3:20; Luke 10:38-42; John 14:23; Matthew 22:37;
1 John 5:14-15; Ephesians 3:18-19; Psalm 139:13; Acts 13:22

Supporting Scripture:

"Here I am! I stand at the door and knock. If anyone hears My voice and opens the door, I will come in and eat with that person, and they with Me."—Revelation 3:20

[38]As Jesus and His disciples were on their way, He came to a village where a woman named Martha opened her home to Him. [39]She had a sister called Mary, who sat at the Lord's feet listening to what He said. [40]But Martha was distracted by all the preparations that had to be made. She came to Him and asked, "Lord, don't You care that my sister has left me to do the work by myself? Tell her to help me!" [41]"Martha, Martha," the Lord answered, "you are worried and upset about many things, [42]but few things are needed—or indeed only one. Mary has chosen what is better, and it will not be taken away from her."—Luke 10:38-42

Jesus replied, "Anyone who loves Me will obey My teaching. My Father will love them, and We will come to them and make Our home with them."—John 14:23

Jesus replied: "'Love the Lord your God with all your heart and with all your soul and with all your mind.'"—Matthew 22:37

[14]This is the confidence we have in approaching God: that if we ask anything according to His will, He hears us. [15]And if we know that He hears us—whatever we ask—we know that we have what we asked of Him.—1 John 5:14-15

[18]may have power, together with all the Lord's holy people, to grasp how wide and long and high and deep is the love of Christ, [19]and to know this love that surpasses knowledge—that you may be filled to the measure of all the fullness of God.—Ephesians 3:18-19

For You created my inmost being; You knit me together in my mother's womb.—Psalm 139:13

After removing Saul, He made David their king. God testified concerning him: 'I have found David son of Jesse, a man after My own heart; he will do everything I want him to do.'—Acts 13:22

Prayer:

Abba Father, make these dead bones come alive for You. Revive my spirit within me. I desire a deeper, more intimate knowledge of You and relationship with You. Please help me establish a practice of meeting with You daily. Let me discern the promptings of Your Spirit within me and then obey. I submit my will to Yours, my heart to Yours, my spirit to Yours. Please make Your Word come alive for me as I read it. Holy Spirit, I want to know You better and hear everything You say. Give me ears to hear You and the heart to obey You. Please make Your home in me. In Jesus' name I pray. Amen.

Personal Reflections:

1) From the **Listen to God** section above, pick out a phrase or two that spoke directly to your heart today. Write the words here:

2) As you re-read and think about the words you wrote above, record any additional words or thoughts that come to your mind:

3) Which of the words or thoughts you recorded above might be from God? Underline or highlight them. Does any Scripture come to mind as you re-read what you've written above? If so, write the portion of Scripture that you recall:

4) Turn to the concordance of your Bible and look up one of the words you recalled from Scripture. Scan the verses cited under the word you have referenced in the concordance and record the references of one or two of the verses that the Holy Spirit illumines with special meaning for you today:

5) Turn to each of the references you recorded above. Read the verse and the surrounding passages. Do any additional words or phrases have special meaning for you today? Perhaps something you needed to hear? Wisdom for a problem you face? An answer to a question? A timely word for a difficult circumstance you currently navigate? If so, record the Scripture or words here:

6) What further question(s) do you have for God today? Write them here:

7) Seek God for answers to the question(s) you wrote above. Ask God one of the questions, and then, sit quietly and wait for His reply. Record the first thought that enters your mind. Write all the thoughts you have as you sit and listen to the Lord:

8) Chances are good that the thoughts you recorded as you sat quietly waiting for the Lord's response were indeed thoughts whispered to you by the Holy Spirit within you. Re-read the thoughts above and ask God to confirm the thoughts that are from Him. Record any new inspirations you hear in your thoughts now:

Identify the Voice:

Re-read the responses you've written to the previous few questions. Run them through the tests below. In each test, the characteristic of God's voice is listed before the OR and the characteristic of Satan's voice is listed after it. Do those thoughts recorded in the section above:

a. Align with the character of God OR the ways of Satan?
b. Agree with the Word of God OR contradict it?
c. Produce the peace of God in your soul OR stir up strife?
d. Convict you OR condemn you?
e. Bring spiritual clarity OR confusion?
f. Offer the Lord's wisdom, instruction, comfort, and encouragement OR cause you to feel doubt, fear, worry, or shame?
g. Bring emotional healing OR cause additional emotional pain?

Using the above tests as your guide, draw a line through any thoughts in the previous section that might be from your enemy, the devil. Take a minute to rebuke Satan aloud. Do not believe his lies or buy in to his accusations or condemnations that you identify in your thoughts.

183

Going Deeper in Two-way Conversation with God:

1) Loving Father, please give me specific ideas, for me personally, on how to establish a regular practice of putting You first, meeting with You. (Write down all the thoughts you receive.)

2) Jesus, fill me with Your love that surpasses knowledge. Speak to my heart today. (Record every word and thought He gives you.)

3) Holy Spirit, please make God's heart known to me. Let me hear Your truth today. (Journal whatever you hear in your heart.)

Review the thoughts God gave you above. Is there a common theme in the impressions you recorded? Perhaps you heard a word that especially warms your heart today? What Scripture comes to mind as you review your notes? Use the concordance of your Bible to look up a word that especially stood out to you or a word that you heard more than once in your thoughts. Scan the list of occurrences of that word cited in Scripture. When you see a verse in the concordance that has special meaning for you today, the Holy Spirit is highlighting that verse for you. Turn to that passage of Scripture and read it. Write the verse here. Then, write all further insights and confirmations the Holy Spirit gives you as you read and ponder God's Word for you today.

Prayer:

Lord, I thank You for creating me and loving me beyond my imagination—beyond what I can grasp and understand. I desire to know You as well as You know me. I want to know Your heart, listen to Your voice, and carry out Your will and plans. Lord, thank You for speaking to me and sharing Your desires. Help me to remain in relationship with You, even as You remain in me. I want to pursue You as passionately as You pursue me. Give me the desire to honor You and please You by sitting at Your feet, listening to every word that falls from Your lips. I love You, Lord, and I want to become a person after Your own heart. In Jesus' precious name I pray. Amen.

Pursuing the Heart of God - Book 2

Day 20 ♥♥ The Will of God

Ask God:

Dear Lord, I want to live the best possible life You have for me. How do I know Your will? What are Your plans for me? When do I need to check with You to make a decision? What direction should I take for this situation? Lord, please let me in on Your will for me.

Listen to God - A Message from His Heart:

My child, *do not live as unwise but as wise; do not be foolish, but understand what My will is for you.* Come to Me for your wisdom. I want you to seek My will in all decisions, in every aspect of your life. I desire your obedience, and in order to obey, you must know My will. *Do not conform to the pattern of this world, but be transformed by the renewing of your mind. Then you will be able to test and approve what My will is—My good, pleasing, and perfect will.*

Renew your mind in My Word. One place you can discover My desired will for you is in the Bible. Read it, believe it, and follow it. Also, when you pray, the Holy Spirit will lead you to Scripture which will instruct you to follow the path I have marked out for you. The Spirit will guide you to the next step in the plans I have pre-determined for you. Seek Me any time, day or night, and I will let you in on My plans for you. *Listen to My voice and follow Me.*

As long as you remain yielded to Me and in communication with Me, I will guide you in My will and provide everything you need to accomplish it. Jesus, My Son, depended on Me and submitted Himself to My will, even unto death on the cross. He did not face that alone. He prayed, *"Father, if You are willing, take this cup from Me; yet not My will but Yours be done."* My will for you is not always the easiest path, but *in all things I work for the good of those who love Me and are called according to My purpose.* Nothing is impossible for Me, and that means *nothing will be impossible for you* when you have faith in Me.

I ask you to trust Me. I am in control. If you think you are in control of your own life, you are deceived. I am in control of all things. However, I do give you the free will to choose. But I know ahead of time what your decision will be, and I work behind the scenes to use it for good. I will continue to work in your life through your circumstances, but it may not be My best for you unless you seek Me first and walk in My will.

That doesn't mean you won't suffer the consequences of your poor decisions. A person reaps what he or she sows. *Whoever sows to please their flesh, from the flesh will reap destruction; whoever sows to please the Spirit, from the Spirit will reap eternal life.* Live by the Spirit, not the flesh. *Keep in step with the Spirit. He guides you along the right paths.*

I know the future, and it is most beneficial for you to seek Me for your next step in all situations. I give you guidance for every step of life. My plans for you are best. Submit yourself to My will, and you will prosper. When you make decisions of your own free will, without consulting Me first, you may suffer the pain of your own making. Do not run ahead of Me. *I act on behalf of those who wait for Me. Hope in Me; you will not be disappointed.*

I know all things, while you have limited knowledge. Making decisions based on your emotions and earthly desires may cause you to step out of My perfect will for you. *Your life is but a mist,* here for a little while and then gone; you do not know if you will see tomorrow. Walk in the favor of My will and lead the best possible life I have for you. *I have come that you may have life, and have it to the full.*

Ephesians 5:15-17; Romans 12:2; John 10:27;
Luke 22:42; Romans 8:28; Matthew 17:20;
Galatians 6:8; Galatians 5:25; Psalm 23:3;
Isaiah 64:4; Isaiah 49:23; James 4:14; John 10:10

Supporting Scripture:

[15]Be very careful, then, how you live—not as unwise but as wise, [16]making the most of every opportunity, because the days are evil. [17]Therefore do not be foolish, but understand what the Lord's will is.—Ephesians 5:15-17

Do not conform to the pattern of this world, but be transformed by the renewing of your mind. Then you will be able to test and approve what God's will is—His good, pleasing and perfect will.— Romans 12:2

"My sheep listen to My voice; I know them, and they follow Me."—John 10:27

"Father, if you are willing, take this cup from Me; yet not My will, but Yours be done."—Luke 22:42

And we know that in all things God works for the good of those who love Him, who have been called according to His purpose.— Romans 8:28

He replied, "Because you have so little faith. Truly I tell you, if you have faith as small as a mustard seed, you can say to this mountain, 'Move from here to there,' and it will move. Nothing will be impossible for you."—Matthew 17:20

[8]Whoever sows to please their flesh, from the flesh will reap destruction; whoever sows to please the Spirit, from the Spirit will reap eternal life.—Galatians 6:8

Since we live by the Spirit, let us keep in step with the Spirit.—Galatians 5:25

He refreshes my soul. He guides me along the right paths for His name's sake.—Psalm 23:3

Since ancient times no one has heard, no ear has perceived, no eye has seen any God besides You, Who acts on behalf of those who wait for Him.—Isaiah 64:4

"...those who hope in Me will not be disappointed."—Isaiah 49:23

Why, you do not even know what will happen tomorrow. What is your life? You are a mist that appears for a little while and then vanishes.—James 4:14

"The thief comes only to steal and kill and destroy; I have come that they may have life, and have it to the full."—John 10:10

Prayer:

Heavenly Father, teach me to do Your will, for You are my God; may Your Spirit lead me and guide me. Help me remember to seek You first, before I make my decisions. Lord, I submit to You and ask You to fill my heart with Your passions and desires. Show me Your plans and guide me in the way You have designed and purposed for me. Let me keep my focus on You and pursue You in such a way that I will receive the reward You have waiting for me. Holy Spirit, share the inner workings of Your heart and Your will with me now. In Jesus' name I pray. Amen.

Personal Reflections:

1) From the **Listen to God** section above, pick out a phrase or two that spoke directly to your heart today. Write the words here:

2) As you re-read and think about the words you wrote above, record any additional words or thoughts that come to your mind:

3) Which of the words or thoughts you recorded above might be from God? Underline or highlight them. Does any Scripture come to mind as you re-read what you've written above? If so, write the portion of Scripture that you recall:

4) Turn to the concordance of your Bible and look up one of the words you recalled from Scripture. Scan the verses cited under the word you have referenced in the concordance and record the references of one or two of the verses that the Holy Spirit illumines with special meaning for you today:

5) Turn to each of the references you recorded above. Read the verse and the surrounding passages. Do any additional words or phrases have special meaning for you today? Perhaps something you needed to hear? Wisdom for a problem you face? An answer to a question? A timely word for a difficult circumstance you currently navigate? If so, record the Scripture or words here:

6) What further question(s) do you have for God today? Write them here:

7) Seek God for answers to the question(s) you wrote above. Ask God one of the questions, and then, sit quietly and wait for His reply. Record the first thought that enters your mind. Write all the thoughts you have as you sit and listen to the Lord:

8) Chances are good that the thoughts you recorded as you sat quietly waiting for the Lord's response were indeed thoughts whispered to you by the Holy Spirit within you. Re-read the thoughts above and ask God to confirm the thoughts that are from Him. Record any new inspirations you hear in your thoughts now:

Identify the Voice:

Re-read the responses you've written to the previous few questions. Run them through the tests below. In each test, the characteristic of God's voice is listed before the OR and the characteristic of Satan's voice is listed after it. Do those thoughts recorded in the section above:

a. Align with the character of God OR the ways of Satan?
b. Agree with the Word of God OR contradict it?
c. Produce the peace of God in your soul OR stir up strife?
d. Convict you OR condemn you?
e. Bring spiritual clarity OR confusion?
f. Offer the Lord's wisdom, instruction, comfort, and encouragement OR cause you to feel doubt, fear, worry, or shame?
g. Bring emotional healing OR cause additional emotional pain?

Using the above tests as your guide, draw a line through any thoughts in the previous section that might be from your enemy, the devil. Take a minute to rebuke Satan aloud. Do not believe his lies or buy in to his accusations or condemnations that you identify in your thoughts.

Going Deeper in Two-way Conversation with God:

1) Lord, is anything in my life blocking my ears from hearing Your voice? If so, please show me the way I have offended You, so that I may remove this roadblock. (Write all words and thoughts He gives you.)

2) Jesus, Your Word lights my way. Please light the next step for me now. (Record whatever you hear from Him.)

3) Holy Spirit, please guide me in the way You would have me go. I commit my way to the Lord; I put my trust in Him. Show me how to live in step with You. (Journal all the thoughts He gives you.)

Review the thoughts God gave you above. Is there a common theme in the impressions you recorded? Perhaps you heard a word that especially warms your heart today? What Scripture comes to mind as you review your notes? Use the concordance of your Bible to look up a word that especially stood out to you or a word that you heard more than once in your thoughts. Scan the list of occurrences of that word cited in Scripture. When you see a verse in the concordance that has special meaning for you today, the Holy Spirit is highlighting that verse for you. Turn to that passage of Scripture and read it. Write the verse here. Then, write all further insights and confirmations the Holy Spirit gives you as you read and ponder God's Word for you today.

Prayer:

Father God Almighty, I will take delight in You. I commit my way to You; I put my trust in You. I will be still and wait patiently for You. You know what is best for me. Lord, please show me Your plans, one step at a time. I desire to do Your will, O God. Give me the forbearance to wait on You and trust in You to give me the full life You intended for me. I want to walk in step with Your Spirit. Let Your Spirit guide my spirit to always remain in step with You. I want You to be the Lord of my life, in all things. In Jesus' name I pray. Amen.

Pursuing the Heart of God - Book 2

Day 21 ♥♥ No More Grumbling or Complaining

Ask God:

Lord, I admit and confess that I grumble and complain too much. I am not as grateful as I should be for all the blessings You have bestowed on me and all the comforts of home and life that You allow me to enjoy. When something does not go right or as I had planned, I confess I am quick to grumble or complain. Please help me understand Your heart with regard to grumbling.

Listen to God - A Message from His Heart:

My beloved one, when you read the story of the Israelites wandering in the desert in Exodus 15-17 and Numbers 14, you see how much they grumbled. I abhor grumbling and complaining. I had rescued My people from 400 years of slavery under Pharaoh; I separated the waters of the Red Sea so they could walk through it; I caused the sea to close up again, killing the Egyptians who pursued the Israelites, saving them again; I had Moses leading them through the desert toward the promised land—a land flowing with milk and honey. And yet they went a few days without good water to drink, and they began grumbling and complaining. A few more days with little food, and they grumbled again, so I provided them daily with manna and quail. They quickly forgot the drudgery they had come from and thought a life of bondage to Pharaoh was better than a life of freedom in Me. I was so frustrated with these ungrateful people that I caused that generation to die in the wilderness after 40 years of wandering. They never made it out of the desert to see the wonderful land I promised them.

You would do well to learn from the mistakes of the Israelite people. Do not practice grumbling and complaining when I have given you so much. Like I freed the Israelites from slavery, I freed you from the bondage and slavery of sin. I gave the life of My one and only Son, Jesus, so that you could live a life of freedom. *Do not worry about your life, what you will eat; or about your body, what you will wear. Seek My kingdom, and these things will be given to you.* I will provide. I always have; I always will. Trust Me to meet all your needs, and quit the grumbling.

In your suffering, you will learn obedience. Instead of complaining, focus on Me and what I have done for you. *Every good and perfect gift is from above.* Raise your prayers and petitions to Me. I hear your cries, and *I know your need before you ask.* However, I still want you to ask Me. *Do not be anxious about anything, but in every situation, by prayer and petition, with thanksgiving, present your requests to Me. And My peace, which transcends all understanding, will guard your heart and mind.*

It is My will that you appreciate all I have given you. *Overflow with thankfulness.* Always show a heart of gratitude for all I continue to do for you. *Rejoice always; pray continually; give thanks in all circumstances.* Trade in your grumbling for thanksgiving. Be thankful and focus on all I have done and continue to do for you. You are My child. I will always love you and take care of you. I am your faithful Father. Be thankful—and no more grumbling!

Luke 12:22, 31; Hebrews 5:8;
James 1:17; Matthew 6:8; Philippians 4:6-7;
Colossians 2:7; 1 Thessalonians 5:16-18

Supporting Scripture:

[22]Then Jesus said to His disciples: "Therefore I tell you, do not worry about your life, what you will eat; or about your body, what you will wear... [31]But seek His kingdom, and these things will be given to you as well."—Luke 12:22, 31

Son though He was, He learned obedience from what He suffered.—Hebrews 5:8

Every good and perfect gift is from above, coming down from the Father of the heavenly lights, Who does not change like shifting shadows.—James 1:17

"Do not be like them, for your Father knows what you need before you ask Him."—Matthew 6:8

[6]Do not be anxious about anything, but in every situation, by prayer and petition, with thanksgiving, present your requests to God. [7]And the peace of God, which transcends all understanding, will guard your hearts and your minds in Christ Jesus.—Philippians 4:6-7

Rooted and built up in Him, strengthened in the faith as you were taught, and overflowing with thankfulness.—Colossians 2:7

[16]Rejoice always, [17]pray continually, [18]give thanks in all circumstances; for this is God's will for you in Christ Jesus.—1 Thessalonians 5:16-18

Prayer:

Heavenly Father, I do appreciate all that You have done for me and for those I love. I give You my thanks and praise Your name. You are continually good to all Your children and Your children's children. You are faithful to generation after generation of those who love You. Lord, I trade in my grumbling for thanksgiving. I am thankful that I can meet with You, one on one, and You will communicate Your heart to me. Holy Spirit, please open my ears to hear Your voice now. In Jesus' name I pray. Amen.

Personal Reflections:

1) From the **Listen to God** section above, pick out a phrase or two that spoke directly to your heart today. Write the words here:

2) As you re-read and think about the words you wrote above, record any additional words or thoughts that come to your mind:

3) Which of the words or thoughts you recorded above might be from God? Underline or highlight them. Does any Scripture come to mind as you re-read what you've written above? If so, write the portion of Scripture that you recall:

4) Turn to the concordance of your Bible and look up one of the words you recalled from Scripture. Scan the verses cited under the word you have referenced in the concordance and record the references of one or two of the verses that the Holy Spirit illumines with special meaning for you today:

5) Turn to each of the references you recorded above. Read the verse and the surrounding passages. Do any additional words or phrases have special meaning for you today? Perhaps something you needed to hear? Wisdom for a problem you face? An answer to a question? A timely word for a difficult circumstance you currently navigate? If so, record the Scripture or words here:

6) What further question(s) do you have for God today? Write them here:

7) Seek God for answers to the question(s) you wrote above. Ask God one of the questions, and then, sit quietly and wait for His reply. Record the first thought that enters your mind. Write all the thoughts you have as you sit and listen to the Lord:

8) Chances are good that the thoughts you recorded as you sat quietly waiting for the Lord's response were indeed thoughts whispered to you by the Holy Spirit within you. Re-read the thoughts above and ask God to confirm the thoughts that are from Him. Record any new inspirations you hear in your thoughts now:

Identify the Voice:

Re-read the responses you've written to the previous few questions. Run them through the tests below. In each test, the characteristic of God's voice is listed before the OR and the characteristic of Satan's voice is listed after it. Do those thoughts recorded in the section above:

a. Align with the character of God OR the ways of Satan?
b. Agree with the Word of God OR contradict it?
c. Produce the peace of God in your soul OR stir up strife?
d. Convict you OR condemn you?
e. Bring spiritual clarity OR confusion?
f. Offer the Lord's wisdom, instruction, comfort, and encouragement OR cause you to feel doubt, fear, worry, or shame?
g. Bring emotional healing OR cause additional emotional pain?

Using the above tests as your guide, draw a line through any thoughts in the previous section that might be from your enemy, the devil. Take a minute to rebuke Satan aloud. Do not believe his lies or buy in to his accusations or condemnations that you identify in your thoughts.

Going Deeper in Two-way Conversation with God:

1) Father God, I confess my ungratefulness in these areas: _____ (fill in the blank). Help me to see the error of my ways and express my thankfulness to You more regularly. Please show me Your heart for me about this. (Write down everything the Lord says to you now.)

2) Jesus, thank You everything You have done for me, especially laying down Your life on my behalf. I also appreciate these things about You: _____ (fill in the blank). How might I best show my appreciation to You? (Record every word and thought you have.)

3) Holy Spirit, I ask that You convict me when I begin to grumble and help me convert that to thanksgiving immediately. Show me how to live a life of thankfulness. What must I do? (Journal all thoughts and ideas He gives you.)

Review the thoughts God gave you above. Is there a common theme in the impressions you recorded? Perhaps you heard a word that especially warms your heart today? What Scripture comes to mind as you review your notes? Use the concordance of your Bible to look up a word that especially stood out to you or a word that you heard more than once in your thoughts. Scan the list of occurrences of that word cited in Scripture. When you see a verse in the concordance that has special meaning for you today, the Holy Spirit is highlighting that verse for you. Turn to that passage of Scripture and read it. Write the verse here. Then, write all further insights and confirmations the Holy Spirit gives you as you read and ponder God's Word for you today.

Prayer:

Lord, please forgive me when I do not appreciate all You have done for me. I should be bouncing off the walls with joy because You have saved me from my sin, and You call me Your child. You gave the life of Your Son so that I could be reconciled to You. I have a roof over my head, food on my table, clothes on my back, and I enjoy good health too. I lack nothing, nor do I need anything. Holy Spirit, next time I want to grumble or complain that something didn't go right, please place a check in my spirit, and help me to find the good in every situation and be thankful for it. In Jesus' precious name I pray. Amen.

Pursuing the Heart of God - Book 2

Day 22 ♥♥ Renew Your Mind

Ask God:

Father in heaven, You have made me a new person in Christ. Purify my heart and revitalize my spirit. I now submit my mind to Your Spirit for complete renewal. Lord, give my mind a makeover, so that I may think and act according to Your will and ways. Lord, let me not focus on the way the world thinks and reasons, but only as You would have me think and reason. Show me what I must do to renew my mind.

Listen to God - A Message from His Heart:

Dear sweet child of Mine—that's what I want you to hear today: You are My child. Your identity in Christ makes you My child—it completes you. You are uniquely you because I created you in My image and yet different than every other person on earth. Your identity as My child gives you access to all of Me and all that I have. You lack nothing.

You were bought at a price, the death of My Son, Jesus Christ. Your redemption was purchased by the blood of Jesus, Who was nailed to a tree for the sin of all humanity. Your identity in Me became secure when you invited Jesus into your heart, confessing Him as your Savior and Lord. I placed My Holy Spirit in your heart. He *marked you as a seal* in Christ; you are My child. The Holy Spirit speaks to you on My behalf, to guide you, comfort you, and give you My wisdom. He reminds you of Scripture and interprets the Word of God for you.

You have been given *the mind of Christ*. One way to renew your mind is to meditate on My Word day and night. Read it, ponder it, digest it, and live it out. You may speak to Me about My Word any time. My Word is *alive and active*. My Spirit will illumine it for you and make it come alive with meaning for every situation you face. Know My wisdom and My will for your life when you spend time in My Word. Discover My character and My love. Hear My instructions and My commands. Allow it to permeate your mind and revitalize your thoughts. *Take captive every thought and make it obedient to Christ.*

Set your mind on what the Spirit desires. The mind governed by the Spirit is life and peace. You are no longer of this world. *Do not conform to it.* You are a stranger to it. Do not live, think, and act as the world does. The world causes you to focus on yourself—put yourself first, take care of yourself, please yourself, do whatever makes you happy. This kind of thinking is opposite of kingdom thinking. I say, put others ahead of yourself. Live as Christ, Who *did not come to be served but to serve.* Humble yourself, and serve others in love.

Do not take care of yourself and live independently from Me, but depend on Me for everything. I desire an intimate relationship with you, which means that you put Me first, seeking Me and My will before you run ahead making your own decisions and your own plans. I desire only the best for your life. Your plans may be good, but are they My best for you? Begin a new practice of seeking Me first in all you do. Refresh your method of operation. Seek Me first. *You will seek Me and find Me when you seek Me with all your heart.*

Allow the Spirit of truth to transform your spiritual heart. You may have believed some words that were not true about yourself. You may have bought into the lies of the enemy, an untrue identity. Let the Spirit expose the lies and replace them with the truth—you are a child of God, you are loved, you are radiant, you are smart, and you are talented. Renew your thoughts with the truth by tuning in to the voice of My Spirit within you. Let Me renew your identity in

Christ. I will refresh your mind and restore your soul. Remain in Me, and be revitalized daily.

1 Corinthians 6:20; Ephesians 1:13; 1 Corinthians 2:16; Hebrews 4:12; 2 Corinthians 10:5; Romans 8:6; Romans 12:2; Matthew 20:28; Jeremiah 29:13

Supporting Scripture:

You were bought at a price. Therefore honor God with your bodies.—1 Corinthians 6:20

And you also were included in Christ when you heard the message of truth, the gospel of your salvation. When you believed, you were marked in Him with a seal, the promised Holy Spirit.—Ephesians 1:13

For "Who has known the mind of the Lord so as to instruct him?" But we have the mind of Christ.—1 Corinthians 2:16

For the Word of God is alive and active. Sharper than any double-edged sword, it penetrates even to dividing soul and spirit, joints and marrow; it judges the thoughts and attitudes of the heart.—Hebrews 4:12

We demolish arguments and every pretension that sets itself up against the knowledge of God, and we take captive every thought to make it obedient to Christ.—2 Corinthians 10:5

The mind governed by the flesh is death, but the mind governed by the Spirit is life and peace.—Romans 8:6

Do not conform to the pattern of this world, but be transformed by the renewing of your mind. Then you will be able to test and approve what God's will is—His good, pleasing and perfect will.—Romans 12:2

"Just as the Son of Man did not come to be served, but to serve, and to give His life as a ransom for many."—Matthew 20:28

"You will seek Me and find Me when you seek Me with all your heart."—Jeremiah 29:13

Prayer:

Heavenly Father, thank You for the gift of the Holy Spirit, Who renews my mind, refreshes my spirit, and restores my soul. You are an awesome Daddy, and I am so blessed to be called Your child. I love You, and I desire to walk with You and talk with You daily. Holy Spirit, please share Your heart with me now regarding my personal circumstances. In Jesus' name I pray. Amen.

Personal Reflections:

1) From the **Listen to God** section above, pick out a phrase or two that spoke directly to your heart today. Write the words here:

2) As you re-read and think about the words you wrote above, record any additional words or thoughts that come to your mind:

3) Which of the words or thoughts you recorded above might be from God? Underline or highlight them. Does any Scripture come to mind as you re-read what you've written above? If so, write the portion of Scripture that you recall:

4) Turn to the concordance of your Bible and look up one of the words you recalled from Scripture. Scan the verses cited under the word you have referenced in the concordance and record the references of one or two of the verses that the Holy Spirit illumines with special meaning for you today:

5) Turn to each of the references you recorded above. Read the verse and the surrounding passages. Do any additional words or phrases have special meaning for you today? Perhaps something you needed to hear? Wisdom for a problem you face? An answer to a question? A timely word for a difficult circumstance you currently navigate? If so, record the Scripture or words here:

6) What further question(s) do you have for God today? Write them here:

7) Seek God for answers to the question(s) you wrote above. Ask God one of the questions, and then, sit quietly and wait for His reply. Record the first thought that enters your mind. Write all the thoughts you have as you sit and listen to the Lord:

8) Chances are good that the thoughts you recorded as you sat quietly waiting for the Lord's response were indeed thoughts whispered to you by the Holy Spirit within you. Re-read the thoughts above and ask God to confirm the thoughts that are from Him. Record any new inspirations you hear in your thoughts now:

Identify the Voice:

Re-read the responses you've written to the previous few questions. Run them through the tests below. In each test, the characteristic of God's voice is listed before the OR and the characteristic of Satan's voice is listed after it. Do those thoughts recorded in the section above:

    a. Align with the character of God OR the ways of Satan?
    b. Agree with the Word of God OR contradict it?
    c. Produce the peace of God in your soul OR stir up strife?
    d. Convict you OR condemn you?
    e. Bring spiritual clarity OR confusion?
    f. Offer the Lord's wisdom, instruction, comfort, and encouragement OR cause you to feel doubt, fear, worry, or shame?
    g. Bring emotional healing OR cause additional emotional pain?

Using the above tests as your guide, draw a line through any thoughts in the previous section that might be from your enemy, the devil. Take a minute to rebuke Satan aloud. Do not believe his lies or buy in to his accusations or condemnations that you identify in your thoughts.

Going Deeper in Two-way Conversation with God:

1) Father God, You have adopted me as Your very own. Please renew my thinking along those lines. Tell me more about my personal and individual identity in Christ. (Record every word you hear.)

2) Jesus, my Savior, You have made me a new creation with the mind of Christ. Please renew my mind and correct my thinking. How do You see me? (Write down all the thoughts He gives you.)

3) Holy Spirit, purify my heart and revitalize my spirit for You. Teach me how to reconnect with You to refresh my thinking and my actions according to God's will. (Journal all the impressions and thoughts He gives you.)

Review the thoughts God gave you above. Is there a common theme in the impressions you recorded? Perhaps you heard a word that especially warms your heart today? What Scripture comes to mind as you review your notes? Use the concordance of your Bible to look up a word that especially stood out to you or a word that you heard more than once in your thoughts. Scan the list of occurrences of that word cited in Scripture. When you see a verse in the concordance that has special meaning for you today, the Holy Spirit is highlighting that verse for you. Turn to that passage of Scripture and read it. Write the verse here. Then, write all further insights and confirmations the Holy Spirit gives you as you read and ponder God's Word for you today.

Prayer:

Dear Jesus, I am grateful for Your Word, Your Spirit, and Your love. Give me the desire to thoughtfully ponder and meditate on Your Word, to connect with Your Spirit, and to understand the depth of Your love for me. Renew my mind, heart, and strength as I pursue a more intimate relationship with You. Thank You for speaking to me daily and refreshing me with Your words of lovingkindness and encouragement. Continue to show me more aspects of Your character and Your heart. In the name of Jesus, my Lord, I pray. Amen.

Pursuing the Heart of God - Book 2

Day 23 ♥♥ Be Humble

Ask God:

Lord, please give me a picture of what it means to be humble. What would You have me do to walk in greater humility? How do You want me to serve others? I confess that I am prideful, and I request that Your Holy Spirit expose my pride every time it surfaces. Help me to see the error of my ways.

Listen to God - A Message from His Heart:

Dear one, I am your Father in heaven, the Sovereign Lord of all, *everlasting God, Creator of the ends of the earth.* I speak and *even the wind and waves obey Me.* I rule and reign over heaven and earth, yet I gave the life of My Son for you. Jesus Christ is the picture of humility. He humbled Himself, taking on flesh of a man, in order to reconcile you to Me so that we could share an intimate relationship. *He came to earth not to be served but to serve.*

Jesus, My Son, bore the weight of all the sins of humankind: past, present, and future; once for all. This is real—it's a personal sacrifice—He humbled Himself and died for your sin. He laid down His life in exchange for yours. He suffered the worst possible death, hanging on a cross—a sentence reserved for the worst of criminals. He did it willingly in obedience to His Father's will. *Greater love has no one than this: to lay down one's life for one's friends.* You are My friend, and My Son did this for you.

I now ask you to do the same: Lay down your life for Me. *Humble yourself, and I will lift you up. Serve one another humbly in love. Value others above yourself, not looking to your own interests but to the interests of others. Set your heart and mind on things above,* not on earthly things of your own desire. *I favor the humble and contrite in spirit.* Clothe yourself with humility toward others, because *I oppose the proud but show favor to the humble.*

In your heart, you make your plans, but it is I, the Lord, Who establishes your steps. Your own plans may fail, but My plans for you are better than you can conceive or imagine. Lay down your pride. Do not be so independent, but be dependent on Me. *I hate pride and arrogance. Pride brings a person low, but the lowly in spirit gain honor.* Sow pride and reap destruction; sow humility and reap honor. *Love Me with all your heart, soul, strength, and mind. Love your neighbor as yourself. Do this and live.* I do not say love yourself only and take pride in yourself, but love Me first with your whole heart, and love others as you have been loved by Me—unconditionally.

Isaiah 40:28; Mark 4:41; Matthew 20:26; John 15:13; James 4:10;
Galatians 5:13; Philippians 2:3-4; Colossians 3:2; Isaiah 66:2;
1 Peter 5:5; Proverbs 16:9; Proverbs 8:13; Proverbs 29:23; Luke 10:27-28

Supporting Scripture:

Do you not know? Have you not heard? The LORD is the everlasting God, the Creator of the ends of the earth. He will not grow tired or weary, and His understanding no one can fathom.—Isaiah 40:28

They were terrified and asked each other, "Who is this? Even the wind and the waves obey Him!"—Mark 4:41

"Not so with you. Instead, whoever wants to become great among you must be your servant, and whoever wants to be first must be your slave—just as the Son of Man did not come to be served, but to serve, and to give His life as a ransom for many."—Matthew 20:26

"Greater love has no one than this: to lay down one's life for one's friends."—John 15:13

Humble yourselves before the Lord, and He will lift you up.—James 4:10.

You, my brothers and sisters, were called to be free. But do not use your freedom to indulge the flesh; rather, serve one another humbly in love."—Galatians 5:13

[3]Do nothing out of selfish ambition or vain conceit. Rather, in humility value others above yourselves, [4]not looking to your own interests but each of you to the interests of the others.—Philippians 2:3-4

Set your minds on things above, not on earthly things.—Colossians 3:2

"…These are the ones I look on with favor: those who are humble and contrite in spirit, and who tremble at My Word."—Isaiah 66:2

In the same way, you who are younger, submit yourselves to your elders. All of you, clothe yourselves with humility toward one another, because, "God opposes the proud but shows favor to the humble."—1 Peter 5:5

In their hearts humans plan their course, but the LORD establishes their steps.—Proverbs 16:9

To fear the LORD is to hate evil; I hate pride and arrogance, evil behavior and perverse speech.—Proverbs 8:13

Pride brings a person low, but the lowly in spirit gain honor.—Proverbs 29:23

[27]He answered, "'Love the Lord your God with all your heart and with all your soul and with all your strength and with all your

mind' and, 'Love your neighbor as yourself.'" [28]"You have answered correctly," Jesus replied, "Do this and you will live."— Luke 10:27-28

Prayer:

Thank You, Lord. I have a better understanding of humility. Please help me walk out Your desires. I submit myself to Your Spirit and ask that He would guide me, convict me, and empower me to live according to Your will. May my words and actions be a beautiful aroma to Your senses. Holy Spirit, please continue to speak to me even more personally now as we meet one on one. Thank You so much. In the name of Jesus Christ, I pray. Amen.

Personal Reflections:

1) From the **Listen to God** section above, pick out a phrase or two that spoke directly to your heart today. Write the words here:

2) As you re-read and think about the words you wrote above, record any additional words or thoughts that come to your mind:

3) Which of the words or thoughts you recorded above might be from God? Underline or highlight them. Does any Scripture come to mind as you re-read what you've written above? If so, write the portion of Scripture that you recall:

4) Turn to the concordance of your Bible and look up one of the words you recalled from Scripture. Scan the verses cited under the word you have referenced in the concordance and record the references of one or two of the verses that the Holy Spirit illumines with special meaning for you today:

5) Turn to each of the references you recorded above. Read the verse and the surrounding passages. Do any additional words or phrases have special meaning for you today? Perhaps something you needed to hear? Wisdom for a problem you face? An answer to a question? A timely word for a difficult circumstance you currently navigate? If so, record the Scripture or words here:

6) What further question(s) do you have for God today? Write them here:

7) Seek God for answers to the question(s) you wrote above. Ask God one of the questions, and then, sit quietly and wait for His reply. Record the first thought that enters your mind. Write all the thoughts you have as you sit and listen to the Lord:

8) Chances are good that the thoughts you recorded as you sat quietly waiting for the Lord's response were indeed thoughts whispered to you by the Holy Spirit within you. Re-read the thoughts above and ask God to confirm the thoughts that are from Him. Record any new inspirations you hear in your thoughts now:

Identify the Voice:

Re-read the responses you've written to the previous few questions. Run them through the tests below. In each test, the characteristic of God's voice is listed before the OR and the characteristic of Satan's voice is listed after it. Do those thoughts recorded in the section above:

a. Align with the character of God OR the ways of Satan?
b. Agree with the Word of God OR contradict it?
c. Produce the peace of God in your soul OR stir up strife?
d. Convict you OR condemn you?
e. Bring spiritual clarity OR confusion?
f. Offer the Lord's wisdom, instruction, comfort, and encouragement OR cause you to feel doubt, fear, worry, or shame?
g. Bring emotional healing OR cause additional emotional pain?

Using the above tests as your guide, draw a line through any thoughts in the previous section that might be from your enemy, the devil. Take a minute to rebuke Satan aloud. Do not believe his lies or buy in to his accusations or condemnations that you identify in your thoughts.

Going Deeper in Two-way Conversation with God:

1) Father, please list some specific ways I have been prideful recently. (Record every thought He gives you.)

2) Jesus, you are the ultimate example of humility. Help me remember all You've done, so that I might live in a similar manner and bring glory to Your name. Lord, in what areas do I need to get rid of pride? (Write everything you think and hear.)

3) Holy Spirit, bring Your conviction upon my heart. I confess that my pride shows through in these ways that You have convicted me with just now:_____ (fill in the blank). Please forgive me and help me live into the new creation You made me when I accepted You as my Savior and Lord.

Review the thoughts God gave you above. Is there a common theme in the impressions you recorded? Perhaps you heard a word that especially warms your heart today? What Scripture comes to mind as you review your notes? Use the concordance of your Bible to look up a word that especially stood out to you or a word that you heard more than once in your thoughts. Scan the list of occurrences of that word cited in Scripture. When you see a verse in the concordance that has special meaning for you today, the Holy Spirit is highlighting that verse for you. Turn to that passage of Scripture and read it. Write the verse here. Then, write all further insights and confirmations the Holy Spirit gives you as you read and ponder God's Word for you today.

Prayer:

Jesus, thank You for humbling Yourself and taking on the nature of a man so that You would be the perfect sacrifice to bring me into a saving relationship with my heavenly Father. Holy Spirit, thank You for exposing my pride. Jesus, please help me to live in Your humility and victory, demonstrated on the cross. As I become the lowly in spirit—the servant—may You become greater and be glorified in me. In Jesus' name I pray. Amen.

Pursuing the Heart of God - Book 2

Day 24 ♥♥ Satan, the Destroyer

Ask God:

Lord, some Christ-followers today do not believe that Satan is still a real threat and influencer. What do You say? Are we really in a daily battle with our enemy, the devil? How do we recognize his attacks? Can we put the blame on him when we sin? How do we discern his voice in our thoughts?

Listen to God - A Message from His Heart:

Child of God, you are a *new creation in Christ Jesus. The old has gone; the new is here!* You may not place blame on Satan for your sin. Satan and sin do not control you unless you allow it. Disobedience is a choice. I have given you the free will to choose right from wrong. It is your decision to obey or disobey Me, to follow My Word or disregard it.

Satan is still a real influencer of humanity against Me. To believe anything less could cost you your life—your marriage, your family, your finances, your friendships, or your relationship with Me. Do not let down your guard. *The thief comes only to steal and kill and destroy, but Jesus came that you may have life in the full.* I have provided you a way out of any temptation by the power of My Holy Spirit in you. Depend on Him; He helps you say no to sin and temptation. Be sensitive to the voice of My Spirit within. *I lead you not into temptation; I deliver you from the evil one.* Your victory belongs to the Lord Christ. Claim the authority of His name and the power of His blood.

Satan speaks to you in your thoughts. He does not know your thoughts, but he interjects his thoughts into your mind. *He leads the whole world astray. He is the accuser,* and his accusations are shaming and condemning. His voice is harsh and condescending. His words are manipulative and wounding. He uses Scripture to deceive, and he distorts the truth. His language is disturbing and confusing. He plants ideas in your mind, trying to keep you from living a life of purity and righteousness in Christ. He will stop at nothing to weaken your faith and damage your relationship with Me, your spouse, your family, your friends—anyone and anything important to you and Me. Remain alert to his ways. He is the destroyer of all good things.

Satan is a liar and the father of lies. He deceives you with altered versions of the truth. When you believe in his lies and give way to his deceit, you take a step toward him and away from Me. You do not want to put yourself in this position, walking down a path to destruction, being *led like a lamb to the slaughter.* No you are victorious. *You are more than a conqueror. Neither death nor life, neither angels nor demons, neither the present nor the future, nor any powers, neither height nor depth, nor anything else in all creation, will be able to separate you from My love that is in Christ Jesus.*

Make no mistake, though. *Be self-controlled and alert. Your enemy the devil prowls around like a roaring lion, looking for someone to devour. Resist him, standing firm in the faith.* Otherwise, your enemy will deceive you and destroy your life. *Your struggle is not against flesh and blood, but against the rulers, against the authorities, against the powers of this dark world and against the spiritual forces of evil in the heavenly realms.* Daily dress yourself in the *full armor of God, so that when the day of evil comes, you may be able to stand your ground, and after you have done everything to stand.* Remember, pray at all times for all My people.

Submit yourself, then, to Me. Resist the devil, and he will flee from you. Come near to Me, and I will come near to you. I have given you My Spirit. You may rely fully on Me. *No temptation will overtake you; I am faithful, I will not allow you to be tempted beyond what you are able but will provide the way of escape also, so that you will be able to endure it. Be strong in Me and in My mighty power.*

2 Corinthians 5:17; John 10:10; Matthew 6:13; Revelation 12:9-10; Isaiah 53:7; John 8:44; Romans 8:37-39; 1 Peter 5:8-9; Ephesians 6:12-13; James 4:7-8; 1 Corinthians 10:13

Supporting Scripture:

Therefore, if anyone is in Christ, the new creation has come: The old has gone, the new is here!—2 Corinthians 5:17

"The thief comes only to steal and kill and destroy; I have come that they may have life, and have it to the full."—John 10:10

"And lead us not into temptation, but deliver us from the evil one."—Matthew 6:13

[9]The great dragon was hurled down—that ancient serpent called the devil, or Satan, who leads the whole world astray. He was hurled to the earth, and his angels with him.[10]Then I heard a loud voice in heaven say: "Now have come the salvation and the power and the kingdom of our God, and the authority of His Messiah. For the accuser of our brothers and sisters, who accuses them before our God day and night, has been hurled down.—Revelation 12:9-10

"...He was a murderer from the beginning, not holding to the truth, for there is no truth in him. When he lies, he speaks his native language, for he is a liar and the father of lies."—John 8:44

He was oppressed and afflicted, yet he did not open his mouth; he was led like a lamb to the slaughter, and as a sheep before its shearers is silent, so he did not open his mouth.—Isaiah 53:7

[37]No, in all these things we are more than conquerors through Him Who loved us. [38]For I am convinced that neither death nor life, neither angels nor demons, neither the present nor the future, nor any powers, [39]neither height nor depth, nor anything else in all creation, will be able to separate us from the love of God that is in Christ Jesus our Lord.—Romans 8:37-39

[8]Be alert and of sober mind. Your enemy the devil prowls around like a roaring lion looking for someone to devour. [9]Resist him, standing firm in the faith, because you know that the family of believers throughout the world is undergoing the same kind of sufferings.—1 Peter 5:8-9

[12]For our struggle is not against flesh and blood, but against the rulers, against the authorities, against the powers of this dark world and against the spiritual forces of evil in the heavenly realms. [13]Therefore put on the full armor of God, so that when the day of evil comes, you may be able to stand your ground, and after you have done everything, to stand.—Ephesians 6:12-13

[7]Submit yourselves, then, to God. Resist the devil, and he will flee from you. [8]Come near to God, and He will come near to you.— James 4:7-8

No temptation has overtaken you except what is common to mankind. And God is faithful; He will not let you be tempted beyond what you can bear. But when you are tempted, He will also provide a way out so that you can endure it.—1 Corinthians 10:13

Prayer:

Heavenly Father, thank You that I can rely on Your Holy Spirit, Your promises, and the truth in Your Word to make choices and decisions according to Your will. Thank You for leading me not into temptation but delivering me from the evil one. Holy Spirit, please make me ultra-sensitive to discerning the thoughts from the devil. When he attempts to lead me astray, remind me of the truth, and help me stand firm in my faith. Spirit, please speak to me now regarding my personal battle with the enemy and how I can be victorious in the daily struggle he engages me in. In Jesus' name I pray. Amen.

Personal Reflections:

1) From the **Listen to God** section above, pick out a phrase or two that spoke directly to your heart today. Write the words here:

2) As you re-read and think about the words you wrote above, record any additional words or thoughts that come to your mind:

3) Which of the words or thoughts you recorded above might be from God? Underline or highlight them. Does any Scripture come to mind as you re-read what you've written above? If so, write the portion of Scripture that you recall:

4) Turn to the concordance of your Bible and look up one of the words you recalled from Scripture. Scan the verses cited under the word you have referenced in the concordance and record the references of one or two of the verses that the Holy Spirit illumines with special meaning for you today:

5) Turn to each of the references you recorded above. Read the verse and the surrounding passages. Do any additional words or phrases have special meaning for you today? Perhaps something you needed to hear? Wisdom for a problem you face? An answer to a question? A timely word for a difficult circumstance you currently navigate? If so, record the Scripture or words here:

6) What further question(s) do you have for God today? Write them here:

7) Seek God for answers to the question(s) you wrote above. Ask God one of the questions, and then, sit quietly and wait for His reply. Record the first thought that enters your mind. Write all the thoughts you have as you sit and listen to the Lord:

8) Chances are good that the thoughts you recorded as you sat quietly waiting for the Lord's response were indeed thoughts whispered to you by the Holy Spirit within you. Re-read the thoughts above and ask God to confirm the thoughts that are from Him. Record any new inspirations you hear in your thoughts now:

Identify the Voice:

Re-read the responses you've written to the previous few questions. Run them through the tests below. In each test, the characteristic of God's voice is listed before the OR and the characteristic of Satan's voice is listed after it. Do those thoughts recorded in the section above:

a. Align with the character of God OR the ways of Satan?
b. Agree with the Word of God OR contradict it?
c. Produce the peace of God in your soul OR stir up strife?
d. Convict you OR condemn you?
e. Bring spiritual clarity OR confusion?
f. Offer the Lord's wisdom, instruction, comfort, and encouragement OR cause you to feel doubt, fear, worry, or shame?
g. Bring emotional healing OR cause additional emotional pain?

Using the above tests as your guide, draw a line through any thoughts in the previous section that might be from your enemy, the devil. Take a minute to rebuke Satan aloud. Do not believe his lies or buy in to his accusations or condemnations that you identify in your thoughts.

Going Deeper in Two-way Conversation with God:

1) Father God, please show me ways the devil is currently attacking me. What are my areas of weakness? (Write down whatever comes to mind just now.)

2) Jesus, it is said, "When I am weak, then I am strong" (see 2 Corinthians 12:10). Please show me how You fortify my weakest walls against my enemy, the devil. What shall I do to protect myself? (Record every word and thought Christ gives you.)

3) Holy Spirit, please identify ways the devil masquerades as an angel of light to me. How am I currently being deceived by him? (Journal all the ideas that run through your mind.)

Review the thoughts God gave you above. Is there a common theme in the impressions you recorded? Perhaps you heard a word that especially warms your heart today? What Scripture comes to mind as you review your notes? Use the concordance of your Bible to look up a word that especially stood out to you or a word that you heard more than once in your thoughts. Scan the list of occurrences of that word cited in Scripture. When you see a verse

in the concordance that has special meaning for you today, the Holy Spirit is highlighting that verse for you. Turn to that passage of Scripture and read it. Write the verse here. Then, write all further insights and confirmations the Holy Spirit gives you as you read and ponder God's Word for you today.

Prayer:

Heavenly Father, thank You that whenever I am tempted, You always give me a way out, by the power of Your Holy Spirit within me. Help me to recognize Your voice and draw on Your assistance every time. I hear You say that I am in a continual battle with the enemy, but I do not always recognize it when I am in the middle of it. Help me to be more sensitive to the devil's deceitful ways and war tactics. Let me engage in battle with the sword of the Spirit, the Word of God, as my weapon of choice. Give me the time to daily read and meditate on Your Word, so that Your Spirit will be able to remind me of it when I need it. Holy Spirit, please bring to my memory the exact Scripture I need, at the exact moment I need it, along with the power and authority to overcome the evil one in the name of Jesus Christ, by His blood. Thank You for the victory over sin, death, and the grave. In the name of Jesus Christ, and by the power of His blood, I ask all this. Amen.

Pursuing the Heart of God - Book 2

Day 25 ♥♥ Spiritual Battle

Ask God:

Lord, there is a daily battle of good vs. evil going on in my mind. I know it, I feel it—it's real. I fight against the desires of the flesh on a daily basis. Holy Spirit, please make me even more sensitive and aware of this, and give me the tools of engagement. Father, make me strong in You. Arm me with Your protective battle suit and defend me against my enemy.

Listen to God - A Message from His Heart:

Child of Mine, you are in a daily spiritual battle—the enemy's goal is to destroy you. Recognizing this is the first step to victory. Whether you realize it or not, there is a conflict raging in you between flesh and Spirit. *Your struggle is not against flesh and blood, but against the rulers, against the authorities, against the powers of this dark world and against the spiritual forces of evil in the heavenly realms.* This battle is as real as you are. It is not a virtual war game. Prepare your method of defense for this war.

Before you put one foot on the floor each morning, dress yourself in My full armor so that you may be able to *stand your ground*. Buckle the *belt of truth* around your waist. The truth is that you are My child, and the devil has no power over you. Believe this truth and claim it. Your identity in Christ gives you the authority over your enemy, as well as the victory over sin, death, and the grave, which the atonement of the shed blood of Jesus Christ on the cross provided for you. Use your authority in the name of Jesus Christ and by the power of His blood to bind up Satan and restrict his destroying influence in your daily life. You are supernaturally empowered by the Spirit of Christ living in you. Be sure to tap in to that amazing power at all times.

Stand firm, then, with the *breastplate of righteousness* in place to avert the flaming arrows of the enemy. He shoots straight for the weakest areas in your heart, but Christ has made you righteous and blameless. Clothing yourself with the breastplate of righteousness, a life of honesty and obedience to God, will keep you pure and ready to stand firm in battle, deflecting all attacks against your standing in Christ. You are Mine, and you have been made righteous in Christ.

Ready yourself to proclaim the *gospel of peace by fitting your feet with My battle sandals*. Anchor yourself in the soil of My salvation and remain steadfast in your faith. Be prepared to share with the lost the message of My love and saving grace. Be a witness for Christ even in the midst of battle. And *take up the shield of faith, with which you can extinguish all the flaming arrows of the evil one*. This is the all-encompassing protection of Christ against everything your enemy hurls at you. Your victory is sure in Jesus' name.

Wear the *helmet of salvation*, putting on the mind of Christ with all wisdom and discernment. *Take up the sword of the Spirit, which is the Word of God*. Do not fight the enemy with your own words and thoughts, but use the Word of God as your weapon of choice. Just as Jesus battled Satan in the wilderness with the Word of God, you too must fight the enemy's lies and deceit with the truth of My Word. As the devil distorts Scripture, you will set him straight with the truth. The power of your testimony is no match for Satan. *You will know the truth, and the truth will set you free*. You are *no longer a slave*, but My child. You have been freed from the bondage of the enemy's lies. Do not return again to a yoke of slavery.

In this world you will have trouble. But take heart! I have overcome the world. You may experience My peace, even in your troubles. *Though you live in the world, you do not wage war as the world does. The weapons you fight with are not the weapons of the world. On the contrary, they have divine power to demolish strongholds. You demolish arguments and every pretension that sets itself up against the knowledge of God, and you take captive every thought to make it obedient to Christ.*

Finally, find your strength in Me. I give you the power and authority you need to overcome the evil one. *Pray in the Spirit on all occasions with all kinds of prayers and requests. With this in mind, be alert and always keep on praying.* Prayer is another strong weapon of warfare. Pray your way through every challenge and struggle. The flesh may be weak, but you are strong in Christ Jesus. *Stand firm, and when you have done everything, remain standing.*

*Ephesians 6:12-18; John 8:32; Galatians 4:7;
John 16:33; 2 Corinthians 10:3-5*

Supporting Scripture:

[12]For our struggle is not against flesh and blood, but against the rulers, against the authorities, against the powers of this dark world and against the spiritual forces of evil in the heavenly realms. [13]Therefore put on the full armor of God, so that when the day of evil comes, you may be able to stand your ground, an after you have done everything to stand. [14]Stand firm then, with the belt of truth buckled around your waist, with the breastplate of righteousness in place, [15]and with your feet fitted with the readiness that comes from the gospel of peace. [16]In addition to all this, take up the shield of faith with which you can extinguish all the flaming arrows of the evil one. [17]Take the helmet of salvation and the sword of the Spirit, which is the Word of God. [18]And pray in the Spirit on all occasions with all kinds of prayers and requests. With this in mind, be alert and always keep on praying for all the Lord's people.—Ephesians 6:12-18

"Then you will know the truth, and the truth will set you free."—John 8:32

So you are no longer a slave, but God's child; and since you are His child, God has made you also an heir.—Galatians 4:7

"I have told you these things, so that in Me you may have peace. In this world you will have trouble. But take heart! I have overcome the world."—John 16:33

^{3}For though we live in the world, we do not wage war as the world does. ^{4}The weapons we fight with are not the weapons of the world. On the contrary, they have divine power to demolish strongholds. ^{5}We demolish arguments and every pretention that sets itself up against the knowledge of God, and we take captive every thought to make it obedient to Christ.—2 Corinthians 10:3-5

Prayer:

Heavenly Father, thank You for being a warrior God; You are my strength and shield. Train me, and prepare me for this daily battle. Holy Spirit, speak to me now with Your words of wisdom, and transform my heart with the truth of Your love and promises. Guard my heart and thoughts. In Jesus' name I pray. Amen.

Personal Reflections:

1) From the **Listen to God** section above, pick out a phrase or two that spoke directly to your heart today. Write the words here:

2) As you re-read and think about the words you wrote above, record any additional words or thoughts that come to your mind:

3) Which of the words or thoughts you recorded above might be from God? Underline or highlight them. Does any Scripture come to mind as you re-read what you've written above? If so, write the portion of Scripture that you recall:

4) Turn to the concordance of your Bible and look up one of the words you recalled from Scripture. Scan the verses cited under the word you have referenced in the concordance and record the references of one or two of the verses that the Holy Spirit illumines with special meaning for you today:

5) Turn to each of the references you recorded above. Read the verse and the surrounding passages. Do any additional words or phrases have special meaning for you today? Perhaps something you needed to hear? Wisdom for a

problem you face? An answer to a question? A timely word for a difficult circumstance you currently navigate? If so, record the Scripture or words here:

6) What further question(s) do you have for God today? Write them here:

7) Seek God for answers to the question(s) you wrote above. Ask God one of the questions, and then, sit quietly and wait for His reply. Record the first thought that enters your mind. Write all the thoughts you have as you sit and listen to the Lord:

8) Chances are good that the thoughts you recorded as you sat quietly waiting for the Lord's response were indeed thoughts whispered to you by the Holy Spirit within you. Re-read the thoughts above and ask God to confirm the

thoughts that are from Him. Record any new inspirations you hear in your thoughts now:

Identify the Voice:

Re-read the responses you've written to the previous few questions. Run them through the tests below. In each test, the characteristic of God's voice is listed before the OR and the characteristic of Satan's voice is listed after it. Do those thoughts recorded in the section above:

a. Align with the character of God OR the ways of Satan?
b. Agree with the Word of God OR contradict it?
c. Produce the peace of God in your soul OR stir up strife?
d. Convict you OR condemn you?
e. Bring spiritual clarity OR confusion?
f. Offer the Lord's wisdom, instruction, comfort, and encouragement OR cause you to feel doubt, fear, worry, or shame?
g. Bring emotional healing OR cause additional emotional pain?

Using the above tests as your guide, draw a line through any thoughts in the previous section that might be from your enemy, the devil. Take a minute to rebuke Satan aloud. Do not believe his lies or buy in to his accusations or condemnations that you identify in your thoughts.

Going Deeper in Two-way Conversation with God:

1) Abba Father, protect me with Your infinite wisdom. Train me in Your warrior ways. Teach me what I need to know for this spiritual battle. (Record everything He says to you.)

2) Jesus, my Deliverer, rescue me from this fight. Do not let me be bound by a yoke of slavery. Please make me aware of what that looks like. (Write all the ideas He gives you.)

3) Holy Spirit, please give me a sense of my most vulnerable weakness, along with the Scripture to fight against the enemy's attack in that area. Prepare me with the Sword of the Spirit, which is the Word of God, so that I am ready to defend myself. (Journal the Scripture that comes to mind. If it's only a word, find the verse in your concordance and write it out here, then meditate on it and memorize it to repeat to the enemy in battle.)

Review the thoughts God gave you above. Is there a common theme in the impressions you recorded? Perhaps you heard a word that especially warms your heart today? What Scripture comes to mind as you review your notes? Use the concordance of your Bible to look up a word that especially stood out to you or a word that you heard more than once in your thoughts. Scan the list of occurrences of that word cited in Scripture. When you see a verse in the concordance that has special meaning for you today, the Holy Spirit is highlighting that verse for you. Turn to that passage of Scripture and read it. Write the verse here. Then, write all further insights and confirmations the Holy Spirit gives you as you read and ponder God's Word for you today.

Prayer:

My Warrior Lord, You do not leave me alone to fight my own battles. You do not allow difficulties to overtake me. You stand with me in the fiery furnace of affliction. You protect me at all times. You give me the victory in every struggle when I depend on You for my strength and wisdom. Strengthen my vulnerable areas, and fortify my weak spots. Deliver me from all my troubles. In the name of Jesus Christ and by His blood shed on the cross, I claim victory over my enemy and bind up the work of Satan, the destroyer. Amen.

Pursuing the Heart of God - Book 2

Day 26 ♥♥ Set Free in Christ

Ask God:

Lord, what does it mean to be set free in Christ? Sometimes I still don't feel free from the power of sin. I want to be free to become all that You created me to be. Lord, how can I claim Your freedom and remain free?

Listen to God - A Message from His Heart:

Child of Mine, when you accepted Christ as your Savior, you became free from the penalty of your sin. Jesus Christ died in your place and paid *the wages of your sin. You are a new creation in Christ Jesus; the old is gone, the new is here.* He has released you from a life of sin. You may now live a life of *righteousness through faith in Christ.* Christ has made you righteous in My eyes, so that we now may enjoy an intimate relationship. You have the freedom to *approach My throne of grace with confidence.*

You were crucified with Christ, so you no longer live, but Christ lives in you. Live by faith in Jesus, Who loved you and gave Himself for you. This may be a difficult concept for you to fully understand. But You accepted Jesus' death as your payment, therefore, you were nailed to the tree with Him. *Your old self was crucified with Him so that the body ruled by sin might be done away with, that you should no longer be a slave to sin—you were set free from it. You are dead to sin but alive to God in Christ. Sin is no longer your master because you are not under the law, but under My grace.*

You are free from the power of sin. *It is for freedom that Christ has set you free. Stand firm, then, and do not let yourself be burdened again by a yoke of slavery.* It is up to you to claim this freedom and walk in the victory over sin that the death of Jesus Christ provided for you. You have the authority of Jesus' name; you have the power of His Spirit within you. You can overcome the desires of the flesh by the power and authority I have given you. *I will not let you be tempted beyond what you can bear, but I will provide a way out.*

I sent My Son to *proclaim good news to the poor, to bind up the brokenhearted, and to proclaim freedom for the captives and release from darkness for the prisoners. He is the Way and the Truth and the Life.* My divine truth has exposed the lies of Satan. The light of My salvation has released you from the bondage of Satan's lies. Do not believe the lies of the enemy when you know the truth of God. Walk in the freedom of the truth. Do not make vows and agreements with the devil when Christ has freed you from the prison of the evil one. Now *you will know the truth, and the truth will set you free. So if the Son sets you free, you will be free indeed.* Claim the freedom of the truth, and walk in it victoriously.

You are free to become what I created you to be. Allow Jesus to live His life in and through you. Be obedient to whatever He asks you to do. He will demonstrate His love and power through you. Do not be distracted by the world, but focus your attention on Christ. Trust Him to live out His perfect will and plan for you, through you. This happens only when you are walking in close relationship with Him through reading the Bible, praying, and listening to His voice. The most important thing you can do is to put Him first, meet with Him daily, talk to Him, and listen to His voice through My Holy Spirit within you.

My Spirit will speak to you in your thoughts and from My Word. The Bible will come alive for you when you tune in to the voice of the Holy Spirit within you. He will remind you of what I say, and He will reveal and interpret Scripture for you, so you are able to understand My wisdom, My promises, and My will for your life.

When you hear and recognize My voice, you experience the life of abundance that Christ came to give you. I want the best for you. I am the best! Be free in Me.

Romans 6:23; 2 Corinthians 5:17; Philippians 3:9; Hebrews 4:16;
Galatians 2:20; Romans 6:6-7, 11, 14; Galatians 5:1;
1 Corinthians 10:13; Isaiah 61:1; John 14:6; John 8:32; John 8:36

Supporting Scripture:

For the wages of sin is death, but the gift of God is eternal life in Christ Jesus our Lord.—Romans 6:23

Therefore, if anyone is in Christ, the new creation has come: The old has gone, the new is here!—2 Corinthians 5:17

And be found in Him, not having a righteousness of my own that comes from the law, but that which is through faith in Christ—the righteousness that comes from God on the basis of faith.— Philippians 3:9

Let us then approach God's throne of grace with confidence, so that we may receive mercy and find grace to help us in our time of need.—Hebrews 4:16

I have been crucified with Christ and I no longer live, but Christ lives in me. The life I now live in the body, I live by faith in the Son of God, Who loved me and gave Himself for me.—Galatians 2:20

[6]For we know that our old self was crucified with Him so that the body ruled by sin might be done away with, that we should no longer be slaves to sin—[7]because anyone who has died has been set free from sin... [11]In the same way, count yourselves dead to sin but alive to God in Christ Jesus...[14]For sin shall no longer be your

master, because you are not under the law, but under grace.—
Romans 6:6-7, 11, 14

It is for freedom that Christ has set us free. Stand firm, then, and do not let yourselves be burdened again by a yoke of slavery.—
Galatians 5:1

No temptation has overtaken you except what is common to mankind. And God is faithful; He will not let you be tempted beyond what you can bear. But when you are tempted, He will also provide a way out so that you can endure it.—1 Corinthians 10:13

The Spirit of the Sovereign LORD is on Me, because the LORD has anointed Me to proclaim good news to the poor. He has sent Me to bind up the brokenhearted, to proclaim freedom for the captives and release from darkness for the prisoners.—Isaiah 61:1

Jesus answered, "I am the way and the truth and the life. No one comes to the Father except through Me."—John 14:6

"Then you will know the truth, and the truth will set you free."—
John 8:32

"So if the Son sets you free, you will be free indeed."—John 8:36

Prayer:

Jesus, my Lord, thank You for dying for me, so that I might live. I submit myself to You and ask that You will live out Your will and plan for me, through me. Allow me to live a life of abundance by clearly hearing Your voice and obeying it. Lord, I am always blessed with so much joy whenever I am obedient to Your requests. Give me the desire to obey Your every command and connect with You daily in two-way conversation. Holy Spirit, speak to me now as we meet to maintain a deeper, more intimate relationship. In Your precious name I pray. Amen.

Personal Reflections:

1) From the **Listen to God** section above, pick out a phrase or two that spoke directly to your heart today. Write the words here:

2) As you re-read and think about the words you wrote above, record any additional words or thoughts that come to your mind:

3) Which of the words or thoughts you recorded above might be from God? Underline or highlight them. Does any Scripture come to mind as you re-read what you've written above? If so, write the portion of Scripture that you recall:

4) Turn to the concordance of your Bible and look up one of the words you recalled from Scripture. Scan the verses cited under the word you have referenced in the concordance and record the references of one or two of the verses that the Holy Spirit illumines with special meaning for you today:

5) Turn to each of the references you recorded above. Read the verse and the surrounding passages. Do any additional words or phrases have special meaning for you today? Perhaps something you needed to hear? Wisdom for a problem you face? An answer to a question? A timely word for a difficult circumstance you currently navigate? If so, record the Scripture or words here:

6) What further question(s) do you have for God today? Write them here:

7) Seek God for answers to the question(s) you wrote above. Ask God one of the questions, and then, sit quietly and wait for His reply. Record the first thought that enters your mind. Write all the thoughts you have as you sit and listen to the Lord:

8) Chances are good that the thoughts you recorded as you sat quietly waiting for the Lord's response were indeed thoughts whispered to you by the Holy Spirit within you. Re-read the thoughts above and ask God to confirm the thoughts that are from Him. Record any new inspirations you hear in your thoughts now:

Identify the Voice:

Re-read the responses you've written to the previous few questions. Run them through the tests below. In each test, the characteristic of God's voice is listed before the OR and the characteristic of Satan's voice is listed after it. Do those thoughts recorded in the section above:

a. Align with the character of God OR the ways of Satan?
b. Agree with the Word of God OR contradict it?
c. Produce the peace of God in your soul OR stir up strife?
d. Convict you OR condemn you?
e. Bring spiritual clarity OR confusion?
f. Offer the Lord's wisdom, instruction, comfort, and encouragement OR cause you to feel doubt, fear, worry, or shame?
g. Bring emotional healing OR cause additional emotional pain?

Using the above tests as your guide, draw a line through any thoughts in the previous section that might be from your enemy, the devil. Take a minute to rebuke Satan aloud. Do not believe his lies or buy in to his accusations or condemnations that you identify in your thoughts.

Going Deeper in Two-way Conversation with God:

1) Heavenly Father, will You expose one area of my life where I remain in the bondage of sin? Please tell me exactly what I need to be free from sin in this area. (Record every

word you hear in your thoughts. Spend some time now confessing your sin and submitting yourself to God.)

2) Jesus, my Savior, please expose one of the enemy's lies that I have believed or bought into, and then set me free with Your truth. (Write down whatever you hear Him say, and claim the freedom He gives you.)

3) Holy Spirit, please show me Your plan for me to live in freedom from the sin and bondage I just confessed. Please remind me of the truth in God's Word and remind me to use it when the enemy attacks me in this area. (Write all the thoughts He gives you on this, and record any words or verses from Scripture that come to mind.)

Review the thoughts God gave you above. Is there a common theme in the impressions you recorded? Perhaps you heard a word that especially warms your heart today? What Scripture comes to mind as you review your notes? Use the concordance of your Bible to look up a word that especially stood out to you or a word that you heard more than once in your thoughts. Scan the list of occurrences of that word cited in Scripture. When you see a verse in the concordance that has special meaning for you today, the Holy Spirit is highlighting that verse for you. Turn to that passage of Scripture and read it. Write the verse here. Then, write all further insights and confirmations the Holy Spirit gives you as you read and ponder God's Word for you today.

Prayer:

Sovereign Lord, Your plans and timing are perfect. I submit my will to Yours and ask that You would live Your life in and through me. Help me become the creation You had in mind when You formed me in the womb. I am grateful that You purchased my freedom from sin and continue to release me from the bondage of sin and the prison of lies I have believed over the years. Lord, I give You access to all areas of my heart and ask that You transform my life so that I might become the creation You called me to be. Holy Spirit, thank You for the abundant blessing I receive by hearing Your voice and living in relationship with You. I am so grateful for everything You do for me. I am blessed to be dead to sin and alive to God in Christ (see Romans 6:11). In the name of Jesus I pray. Amen.

Pursuing the Heart of God - Book 2

Day 27 ♥♥ Strength in Weakness

Ask God:

Heavenly Father, sometimes I feel so physically, emotionally, and spiritually drained. I am spent. I cannot even muster enough strength to take the next step, to put one foot in front of the other. Lord, where do I turn from here? Where do I find my strength in weakness? Why do I feel so weak? I am so humbled at this point. I have lost all my strength and independence.

Listen to God - A Message from His Heart:

My dear child, let Me explain. In order to keep you from being prideful, I allow trials and challenges in your life. When you are humbled before Me and emptied of all your pride, when you reach the end of yourself, only then are you ready to receive My grace and help. You begin to understand that everything you hold closely, and all that you are, comes from My hand. *Every good and perfect gift is from above.* I see you in your weakness and give you My strength.

Pain, grief, disappointment, rejection, and failure may bring you to your knees. That is not a bad place to be. I often need to allow these tough times in your life before you are ready to let go and let Me begin to go to work for you. I promise that *in all things I work for the good of those who love Me and are called according to My purpose.* If you never experienced frailty, would you ever have a need for Me? My desire is that you will run to Me in these tough times, so I might teach you about My love and faithfulness. However, I would love for you to seek Me in the good times as well. Worship Me and *seek Me with your whole heart. Love Me with all your heart, soul, and strength.* Put Me first, above everything else.

Depend on Me. *When you are weak, it is then you are strong* in Me. *Therefore, be willing to boast all the more gladly about your weaknesses. My power is made perfect in weakness.* Your weakness is My strength. Believe it! *You can do all things through Christ, Who strengthens you.* You will know My strength when you remain in relationship with Me, especially when you are at your lowest point. In difficult times, *I am your Rock and your Fortress.* I am all that you need.

Do not fear; I am with you. I will strengthen you and help you. I am with you in all your trials, every one. *I will never leave you nor forsake you.* I wait patiently for you to turn to Me for help and strength. My arms are always open to you. Run to Me when you are exhausted. *I will renew your strength, and you will soar on wings like eagles; you will run and not grow weary, walk and not grow faint.* I am here for you, My child. You have access to all that is Mine, including My strength, at all times. Just ask!

James 1:17; Romans 8:28; Deuteronomy 4:29; Deuteronomy 6:5;
2 Corinthians 12:9-10; Philippians 4:13; Psalm 18:2;
Isaiah 41:10; Joshua 1:5; Isaiah 40:31

Supporting Scripture:

Every good and perfect gift is from above, coming down from the Father of the heavenly lights, Who does not change like shifting shadows.—James 1:17

And we know that in all things God works for the good of those who love Him, who have been called according to His purpose.—Romans 8:28

But if from there you seek the LORD your God, you will find Him if you seek Him with all your heart and with all your soul.—Deuteronomy 4:29

Love the LORD your God with all your heart and with all your soul and with all your strength.—Deuteronomy 6:5

⁹But He said to me, "My grace is sufficient for you, for My power is made perfect in weakness." Therefore I will boast all the more gladly about my weaknesses, so that Christ's power may rest on me. ¹⁰That is why, for Christ's sake, I delight in weaknesses, in insults, in hardships, in persecutions, in difficulties. For when I am weak, then I am strong.—2 Corinthians 12:9-10

I can do all this through Him Who gives me strength.—Philippians 4:13

The LORD is my rock, my fortress, and my deliverer; my God is my rock, in whom I take refuge, my shield and the horn of my salvation, my stronghold.—Psalm 18:2

"So do not fear, for I am with you; do not be dismayed, for I am your God. I will strengthen you and help you; I will uphold you with My righteous right hand."—Isaiah 41:10

"No one will be able to stand against you all the days of your life. As I was with Moses, so I will be with you; I will never leave you nor forsake you."—Joshua 1:5

But those who hope in the LORD will renew their strength. They will soar on wings like eagles; they will run and not grow weary, they will walk and not be faint.—Isaiah 40:31

Prayer:

Father in heaven, I am in awe of You. You are so good to Me. You are always there for Me any time I need a helping hand, a word of encouragement, a boost in my spirit. Thank You for Your lovingkindness and Your faithfulness. I can do all things through Christ, Who strengthens me (see Philippians 4:13). I am thankful in the trials because I can depend on You. Holy Spirit, please speak to me from Your heart at this time. In the name of Christ, my solid Rock, I pray. Amen.

Personal Reflections:

1) From the **Listen to God** section above, pick out a phrase or two that spoke directly to your heart today. Write the words here:

2) As you re-read and think about the words you wrote above, record any additional words or thoughts that come to your mind:

3) Which of the words or thoughts you recorded above might be from God? Underline or highlight them. Does any Scripture come to mind as you re-read what you've written above? If so, write the portion of Scripture that you recall:

4) Turn to the concordance of your Bible and look up one of the words you recalled from Scripture. Scan the verses cited under the word you have referenced in the concordance and record the references of one or two of the verses that the Holy Spirit illumines with special meaning for you today:

5) Turn to each of the references you recorded above. Read the verse and the surrounding passages. Do any additional words or phrases have special meaning for you today? Perhaps something you needed to hear? Wisdom for a problem you face? An answer to a question? A timely word for a difficult circumstance you currently navigate? If so, record the Scripture or words here:

6) What further question(s) do you have for God today? Write them here:

7) Seek God for answers to the question(s) you wrote above. Ask God one of the questions, and then, sit quietly and wait for His reply. Record the first thought that enters your mind. Write all the thoughts you have as you sit and listen to the Lord:

8) Chances are good that the thoughts you recorded as you sat quietly waiting for the Lord's response were indeed thoughts whispered to you by the Holy Spirit within you. Re-read the thoughts above and ask God to confirm the thoughts that are from Him. Record any new inspirations you hear in your thoughts now:

Identify the Voice:

Re-read the responses you've written to the previous few questions. Run them through the tests below. In each test, the characteristic of God's voice is listed before the OR and the characteristic of Satan's voice is listed after it. Do those thoughts recorded in the section above:

a. Align with the character of God OR the ways of Satan?
b. Agree with the Word of God OR contradict it?
c. Produce the peace of God in your soul OR stir up strife?
d. Convict you OR condemn you?
e. Bring spiritual clarity OR confusion?

f. Offer the Lord's wisdom, instruction, comfort, and encouragement OR cause you to feel doubt, fear, worry, or shame?

g. Bring emotional healing OR cause additional emotional pain?

Using the above tests as your guide, draw a line through any thoughts in the previous section that might be from your enemy, the devil. Take a minute to rebuke Satan aloud. Do not believe his lies or buy in to his accusations or condemnations that you identify in your thoughts.

Going Deeper in Two-way Conversation with God:

1) Papa God, what is it that You want me to know and hear from You today? (Record all the thoughts He gives you.)

2) Jesus, my Fortress and my Deliverer, renew my strength today. Speak to me from Your heart. (Write every word you hear from Him.)

3) Holy Spirit, lead me to the Word of God I need to hear today. Please encourage me in my weakness. (Journal the words and ideas He gives you.)

Review the thoughts God gave you above. Is there a common theme in the impressions you recorded? Perhaps you heard a word that especially warms your heart today? What Scripture comes to mind as you review your notes? Use the concordance of your Bible to look up a word that especially stood out to you or a word that you heard more than once in your thoughts. Scan the list of occurrences of that word cited in Scripture. When you see a verse in the concordance that has special meaning for you today, the Holy Spirit is highlighting that verse for you. Turn to that passage of Scripture and read it. Write the verse here. Then, write all further insights and confirmations the Holy Spirit gives you as you read and ponder God's Word for you today.

Prayer:

Loving Father, thank You for Your kind words and faithful promises. I am so blessed to have You for my Papa. I owe my life to You; You are my Strength and my All in All. Thank You for renewing my strength when I am weak, even for carrying me in the difficult times. You build me up when I am frail. You lift me up when I am down. You support me in all I do. I love You with all my heart, soul, mind, and strength. In Jesus' name I pray. Amen.

Pursuing the Heart of God - Book 2

Day 28 ♥♥ Full Obedience

Ask God:

Father God, the word 'obey' is perceived so negatively in society and is so contrary to the ways of the world. Sometimes we fear what You will ask of us. How do You see obedience?

Listen to God - A Message from His Heart:

My child, do not tremble at the word 'obey.' I will always enable you and empower you to do whatever I ask of you. I know what is best for you, and I would not ask you to do anything outside of My will. I am the Sovereign God; I rule and reign over all. Believe Me. *I have the power to do what I promise.* You can trust in Me to do what is in your best interest. Submit yourself to My authority and My instructions. Trust in Me and obey My commands.

Do not let your fear keep you from listening to My voice and obeying. As I commanded Joshua, so I encourage you: *Be strong and courageous! I am with you wherever you go.* Your obedience may cause you to face some challenges in unknown places, but I am with you always, leading you on your way. I will fight for you and die for you. You have seen My promises fulfilled.

I am the omniscient Father. In all things, I know the perfect timing. Do not rush ahead on your own, in your own timing, but wait on Me. *I act on behalf of the one who waits for Me.* Tune in to My Spirit within and be sensitive to His voice. He will show you when to move and when to stay. *Walk in obedience to all I command you so that it may go well with you.*

Seek Me in the morning, and I will show you My will for your day. Put your trust in Me. I will lead you each step of the way in the plans I have for you. I may not show you more than the next step ahead. You may not have full understanding of the course I lead you on, but I will guide you down the path I have marked out for you. You may experience conflicts or objections from others as you seek to obey My will. *You must obey Me rather than humans.* I am Lord of all. I see and know the future. I do what is best for your future. Trust Me with all your steps, even when you know not one of them. Be sensitive to My Spirit within. He will lead you in the way that leads to life eternal.

On the other hand, disobedience brings consequence, even death. Continual disobedience is rebellion. This is not a good path to walk down. When you fall short of My will, be quick to confess and repent. Partial obedience is also rebellion. Full obedience is to do what I ask, how I ask you to do it, when I say to do it. Anything less than this is not obedience. I am not pleased with partial obedience. I love you, and I want you to receive the blessings that follow your full obedience to Me.

Take the same attitude as Jesus did when He said, *"Yet not My will, but Yours be done."* Where would you be if Jesus had not obeyed My will and gone to the cross? There would be no escape from the payment of your sin—the death penalty. There would be no reconciliation with Me. You would remain in your sin and reap the just punishment, eternal separation from Me. I do not ask you to do anything I have not done Myself. Be obedient to My will and see it through to the end.

I hear your prayers and petitions because of your reverent submission, and you will learn obedience from your suffering, even as Christ Himself *learned obedience from what He suffered. You know Me if you keep My commands. If anyone obeys My Word, love for Me is truly made complete in them. Whoever claims to live in Me must live as Jesus did.* When you love Me, you will obey Me. *When you obey Me, I will love you and make My home in you.*

Meditate on My Word day and night, and be careful to do everything written in it. Do not merely listen to the Word and so deceive yourselves. Do what it says. When you read My Word, do not quit there. Carefully think about what it says and what I might be saying to you in the moment. My Spirit will illumine Scripture for you that is pertinent to a current circumstance you walk in.

Blessed are those who hear the Word of God and obey it. Do not merely hear the Word, but also submit to it and act on it. Stay in tune with My Spirit and do what I command. Nourish your soul with obedience to Me. Find My joy in your obedience; I always bless you when you follow My instructions. Show Me your love by the act of obedience to all I command you. I want only the best for you in all you do.

Romans 4:21; Joshua 1:9; Isaiah 64:4; Jeremiah 7:23;
Acts 5:29; Luke 22:42; Hebrews 5:8; 1 John 2:3-6;
John 14:23; Joshua 1:8; James 1:22; Luke 11:28

Supporting Scripture:

"Being fully persuaded that God had power to do what He had promised."—Romans 4:21

"Have I not commanded you? Be strong and courageous. Do not be afraid; do not be discouraged, for the LORD your God will be with you wherever you go."—Joshua 1:9

Since ancient times no one has heard, no ear has perceived, no eye has seen any God besides You, Who acts on behalf of those who wait for Him.—Isaiah 64:4

"But I gave them this command: Obey Me, and I will be your God and you will be My people. Walk in obedience to all I command you, that it may go well with you."—Jeremiah 7:23

Peter and the other apostles replied: "We must obey God rather than human beings."—Acts 5:29

"Father, if You are willing, take this cup from Me; yet not My will, but Yours be done."—Luke 22:42

Son though He was, He learned obedience from what He suffered.—Hebrews 5:8

[3]We know that we have come to know Him if we keep His commands. [4]Whoever says, "I know Him, but does not do what He commands is a liar, and the truth is not in that person. [5]But if anyone obeys His Word, love for God is truly made complete in them. This is how we know we are in Him: [6]Whoever claims to live in Him must live as Jesus did.—1 John 2:3-6

Jesus replied, "Anyone who loves Me will obey My teaching. My Father will love them, and We will come to them and make Our home with them."—John 14:23

Keep this Book of the Law always on your lips; meditate on it day and night, so that you may be careful to do everything written in it. Then you will be prosperous and successful.—Joshua 1:8

Do not merely listen to the Word, and so deceive yourselves. Do what it says.—James 1:22

He replied, "Blessed rather are those who hear the Word of God and obey it."—Luke 11:28

Prayer:

Heavenly Father, not My will but Yours be done. I know You have my best in mind, and what You have planned is best. Lord, I submit my will to Yours and ask that Your Holy Spirit will help me and empower me to carry out whatever You ask of me. Spirit of

God, please speak to me more personally right now, and allow me to see the next step in the path You have ordained for me. In Jesus' name I pray. Amen.

Personal Reflections:

1) From the **Listen to God** section above, pick out a phrase or two that spoke directly to your heart today. Write the words here:

2) As you re-read and think about the words you wrote above, record any additional words or thoughts that come to your mind:

3) Which of the words or thoughts you recorded above might be from God? Underline or highlight them. Does any Scripture come to mind as you re-read what you've written above? If so, write the portion of Scripture that you recall:

4) Turn to the concordance of your Bible and look up one of the words you recalled from Scripture. Scan the verses cited under the word you have referenced in the concordance and record the references of one or two of the verses that the Holy Spirit illumines with special meaning for you today:

5) Turn to each of the references you recorded above. Read the verse and the surrounding passages. Do any additional words or phrases have special meaning for you today? Perhaps something you needed to hear? Wisdom for a problem you face? An answer to a question? A timely word for a difficult circumstance you currently navigate? If so, record the Scripture or words here:

6) What further question(s) do you have for God today? Write them here:

7) Seek God for answers to the question(s) you wrote above. Ask God one of the questions, and then, sit quietly and wait for His reply. Record the first thought that enters your mind. Write all the thoughts you have as you sit and listen to the Lord:

8) Chances are good that the thoughts you recorded as you sat quietly waiting for the Lord's response were indeed thoughts whispered to you by the Holy Spirit within you.

Re-read the thoughts above and ask God to confirm the thoughts that are from Him. Record any new inspirations you hear in your thoughts now:

Identify the Voice:

Re-read the responses you've written to the previous few questions. Run them through the tests below. In each test, the characteristic of God's voice is listed before the OR and the characteristic of Satan's voice is listed after it. Do those thoughts recorded in the section above:

   a. Align with the character of God OR the ways of Satan?
   b. Agree with the Word of God OR contradict it?
   c. Produce the peace of God in your soul OR stir up strife?
   d. Convict you OR condemn you?
   e. Bring spiritual clarity OR confusion?
   f. Offer the Lord's wisdom, instruction, comfort, and encouragement OR cause you to feel doubt, fear, worry, or shame?
   g. Bring emotional healing OR cause additional emotional pain?

Using the above tests as your guide, draw a line through any thoughts in the previous section that might be from your enemy, the devil. Take a minute to rebuke Satan aloud. Do not believe his lies or buy in to his accusations or condemnations that you identify in your thoughts.

Going Deeper in Two-way Conversation with God:

1) Sovereign God, You see the big picture; You know the future. What is Your will for me? What is the next step required of me to be obedient to it? (Record everything you hear Him say.)

2) Jesus, You are the ultimate model of submission and obedience to the Father's will. Please share with me how to have the same attitude that You achieved in the most difficult circumstances. (Write down all the words and thoughts He brings to your mind.)

3) Holy Spirit, empower me to do the will of the Father. Teach me to hear and know Your voice so that I might be able to understand what is asked of me and rely on Your power to accomplish it. What do You want me to hear right now? (Journal all ideas and impressions the Holy Spirit gives to you.)

Review the thoughts God gave you above. Is there a common theme in the impressions you recorded? Perhaps you heard a word that especially warms your heart today? What Scripture comes to mind as you review your notes? Use the concordance of your Bible to look up a word that especially stood out to you or a word that you heard more than once in your thoughts. Scan the list of occurrences of that word cited in Scripture. When you see a verse in the concordance that has special meaning for you today, the Holy Spirit is highlighting that verse for you. Turn to that passage of Scripture and read it. Write the verse here. Then, write all further insights and confirmations the Holy Spirit gives you as you read and ponder God's Word for you today.

Prayer:

Father God, You are wise and wonderful. I trust Your will and plans for me are perfect, no matter the cost or difficulty. I submit myself to Your will. I ask you to prepare me, equip me, empower me to be obedient and accomplish all that You created me for. I want to bring glory to Your name. I ask this in the name of Jesus Christ, my Lord. Amen.

Pursuing the Heart of God - Book 2

Day 29 ♥♥ Fruit of the Spirit

Ask God:

Lord, displaying the fruit of the Spirit seems a goal too difficult to continually attain. How do I become a fruit-bearing Christian? How do I maintain a life of fruitfulness in You? Lord, may You be known by the fruit of the Spirit displayed in me. I want to serve You and bring You glory all the days of my life. Let me be known as Your disciple by Your good fruit in me.

Listen to God - A Message from His Heart:

My sweet child, I desire a close relationship with you. When you remain continually connected to Me, My Spirit produces His good fruit in you. You cannot yield the fruit of the Spirit on your own. You must submit yourself to the purifying work of the Holy Spirit. The Spirit produces choice fruit in you; it is not the result of your own doing. Be the bearer of good fruit. *Walk by the Spirit*, staying in step with Him rather than striving in the flesh. Depend on Me and be sensitive to the promptings of the Spirit within.

The Holy Spirit is continually sanctifying you; daily He transforms you into the image of Christ Jesus. Surrender your will to Him. Pay attention to His voice. *Walk by the Spirit, and you will not gratify the desires of the flesh. Crucify the flesh with its passions and desires, and live by the Spirit, keeping in step with Him at all times.* When you do this, you *will be recognized by your fruit. Every good tree bears good fruit, but a bad tree bears bad fruit.* You are a good tree when you remain rooted in Me.

Meditate on My Word day and night, and you will be like a tree planted by streams of water, which yields its fruit in season and whose leaf does not wither—whatever you do will prosper. Blessed are you when you trust in the Lord and put your confidence in Him. You will be like a *tree planted by the water that sends out its roots by the stream. It does not fear when heat comes; its leaves are always green. It has no worries in a year of drought and never fails to bear fruit.*

Ask Me, and I will fill you with the knowledge of My will through all the wisdom and understanding that My Spirit gives, so that you may live a life worthy of Me and please Me in every way: bearing fruit in every good work. Ask, and you will receive. Know My will, and live in it. Remain in Me, and the Spirit will make you fruitful in all your works.

You are known to be My disciple when you display the fruit of the Spirit in both your words and your deeds. Stay tuned into My Spirit. When you remain in relationship with Me, you will experience My love, joy, and peace. The seed I sow in you will reap a harvest of fruitfulness in you for others to *taste and see that I am good.* When you have experienced My patience, kindness, and goodness, you can't help but display it and share it with others. Surrender to the control of My Spirit, and *clothe yourself with compassion, kindness, humility, gentleness, and patience. Bear with each other, and forgive one another as I have forgiven you. Let your love bind all these virtues together, and let peace rule in your heart.*

Remain in Me, as I also remain in you. You cannot bear fruit on your own; You must remain in daily connection with Me. *If you remain in Me and I in you, you will bear much fruit; apart from Me, you can do nothing. You did not choose Me, but I chose you and appointed you so that you might go and bear fruit—fruit that will last—and so that whatever you ask in My name the Father will give you.* Be transformed by My Spirit as you live in step with Him, and you will bear fruit that will last.

Galatians 5:16; Galatians 5:24-25; Matthew 12:33;
Matthew 7:17, 20; Psalm 1:2-3; Jeremiah 17:7-8;
Colossians 1:9-10; Psalm 34:8; Colossians 3:12-14; John 15:4,16

Supporting Scripture:

So I say, walk by the Spirit, and you will not gratify the desires of the flesh.—Galatians 5:16

[24]Those who belong to Christ Jesus have crucified the flesh with its passions and desires. [25]Since we live by the Spirit, let us keep in step with the Spirit.—Galatians 5:24-25

"Make a tree good and its fruit will be good, or make a tree bad and its fruit will be bad, for a tree is recognized by its fruit."—Matthew 12:33

[17]"Likewise, every good tree bears good fruit, but a bad tree bears bad fruit... [20]Thus, by their fruit you will recognize them."—Matthew 7:17, 20

[2]but whose delight is in the law of the LORD, and who meditates on His law day and night. [3]That person is like a tree planted by streams of water, which yields its fruit in season and whose leaf does not wither—whatever they do prospers.—Psalm 1:2-3

[7]"But blessed is the one who trusts in the LORD, whose confidence is in Him. [8]They will be like a tree planted by the water that sends out its roots by the stream. It does not fear when heat comes; its leaves are always green. It has no worries in a year of drought and never fails to bear fruit."—Jeremiah 17:7-8

[9]For this reason, since the day we heard about you, we have not stopped praying for you. We continually ask God to fill you with the knowledge of His will through all the wisdom and understanding that the Spirit gives, [10]so that you may live a life worthy of the Lord and please Him in every way: bearing fruit in

every good work, growing in the knowledge of God.—Colossians 1:9-10

Taste and see that the L ORD is good; blessed is the one who takes refuge in Him.—Psalm 34:8

[12]Therefore, as God's chosen people, holy and dearly loved, clothe yourselves with compassion, kindness, humility, gentleness and patience. [13]Bear with each other and forgive one another if any of you has a grievance against someone. Forgive as the Lord forgave you. [14]And over all these virtues put on love, which binds them all together in perfect unity.—Colossians 3:12-14

[4]"Remain in Me, as I also remain in you. No branch can bear fruit by itself; it must remain in the vine. Neither can you bear fruit unless you remain in Me... [16]You did not choose Me, but I chose you and appointed you so that you might go and bear fruit—fruit that will last—and so that whatever you ask in My name the Father will give you."—John 15:4, 16

Prayer:

Dear Heavenly Father, I do want to glorify Your holy name. I ask that Your Spirit purify me and transform me into the image of Jesus Christ. I pray that I can remain in an intimate relationship with You, walking in step with the Spirit, so that I will become a good tree that produces choice fruit. Holy Spirit, I submit myself to Your transforming power so that I will blossom. Mature those blossoms into vine-ripened fruit. Let me remain in the Vine right now, as we speak face to face in quiet conversation. In Jesus' name I pray. Amen.

Personal Reflections:

1) From the **Listen to God** section above, pick out a phrase or two that spoke directly to your heart today. Write the words here:

2) As you re-read and think about the words you wrote above, record any additional words or thoughts that come to your mind:

3) Which of the words or thoughts you recorded above might be from God? Underline or highlight them. Does any Scripture come to mind as you re-read what you've written above? If so, write the portion of Scripture that you recall:

4) Turn to the concordance of your Bible and look up one of the words you recalled from Scripture. Scan the verses cited under the word you have referenced in the concordance and record the references of one or two of the verses that the Holy Spirit illumines with special meaning for you today:

5) Turn to each of the references you recorded above. Read the verse and the surrounding passages. Do any additional words or phrases have special meaning for you today? Perhaps something you needed to hear? Wisdom for a problem you face? An answer to a question? A timely word for a difficult circumstance you currently navigate? If so, record the Scripture or words here:

6) What further question(s) do you have for God today? Write them here:

7) Seek God for answers to the question(s) you wrote above. Ask God one of the questions, and then, sit quietly and wait for His reply. Record the first thought that enters your mind. Write all the thoughts you have as you sit and listen to the Lord:

8) Chances are good that the thoughts you recorded as you sat quietly waiting for the Lord's response were indeed thoughts whispered to you by the Holy Spirit within you. Re-read the thoughts above and ask God to confirm the thoughts that are from Him. Record any new inspirations you hear in your thoughts now:

Identify the Voice:

Re-read the responses you've written to the previous few questions. Run them through the tests below. In each test, the characteristic of God's voice is listed before the OR and the characteristic of Satan's voice is listed after it. Do those thoughts recorded in the section above:

a. Align with the character of God OR the ways of Satan?
b. Agree with the Word of God OR contradict it?
c. Produce the peace of God in your soul OR stir up strife?
d. Convict you OR condemn you?
e. Bring spiritual clarity OR confusion?
f. Offer the Lord's wisdom, instruction, comfort, and encouragement OR cause you to feel doubt, fear, worry, or shame?
g. Bring emotional healing OR cause additional emotional pain?

Using the above tests as your guide, draw a line through any thoughts in the previous section that might be from your enemy, the devil. Take a minute to rebuke Satan aloud. Do not believe his lies or buy in to his accusations or condemnations that you identify in your thoughts.

Going Deeper in Two-way Conversation with God:

1) Father God, please share from Your heart what I need to improve on to maintain a more cherished relationship with You. (Write whatever you hear Him say.)

2) Jesus, my Friend, You are the Vine, and I am the branch. How do I bear fruit that will last? What is my part in this command? (Record everything Christ says to you in your thoughts.)

3) Holy Spirit, help me stay in step with You. Allow me to hear Your voice clearly. What am I missing? What must I do to remain in step with You? (Journal your thoughts and the impressions He gives you now.)

Review the thoughts God gave you above. Is there a common theme in the impressions you recorded? Perhaps you heard a word that especially warms your heart today? What Scripture comes to mind as you review your notes? Use the concordance of your Bible to look up a word that especially stood out to you or a word that you heard more than once in your thoughts. Scan the list of occurrences of that word cited in Scripture. When you see a verse in the concordance that has special meaning for you today, the Holy Spirit is highlighting that verse for you. Turn to that passage of Scripture and read it. Write the verse here. Then, write all further insights and confirmations the Holy Spirit gives you as you read and ponder God's Word for you today.

Prayer:

Jesus, My Savior, You laid down Your life for me. I want to honor You by laying down the desires of the flesh and picking up my cross daily to follow You. I submit my will to Yours and ask that Your Spirit empower me to live a fruitful life when I remain in close relationship with You. As I read and meditate on Your Word, let me bear fruit as I remain in You and You remain in me. In the name of Jesus I pray. Amen.

Pursuing the Heart of God - Book 2

Day 30 ♥♥ Spiritual Growth

Ask God:

Heavenly Father, You have saved me and called me to grow in the grace and knowledge of the Lord Jesus Christ (see 2 Peter 3:18). Teach me the best ways to mature in You, grow in my faith, and bear much fruit for Your glory. I am wholly Yours. Holy Spirit, transform me into the image of God's Son, Jesus Christ, so I may live a life that pleases Him.

Listen to God - A Message from His Heart:

My faithful child, you have already been given everything you need to become like Jesus Christ in every way. The One Who saved you and gave you His Spirit is able to teach you how to live a life that pleases Me. You have been given a new life in Jesus Christ. *All things are possible through Him Who strengthens you.*

It is up to you to tap into that divine power in Christ Jesus. Allow Jesus to live His life in and through you. Abandon sin, and rely on the life-giving power of Jesus Christ through the Holy Spirit living in you. Make Jesus the Lord of your life. Read My Word and listen for the voice of My Spirit within you. He will guide you on an exciting journey of faith and adventure in Christ. Grow and mature in your relationship with Me by spending time in My Word and obeying the instructions you hear from My lips. *Grow in the grace and knowledge of the Lord Jesus Christ.* Grow in relationship with Me, and become even more fruitful.

My Holy Spirit gives you everything you need to live a godly life. Live in step with the Spirit and *make every effort to add to your faith goodness; and to goodness, knowledge; and to knowledge,*

274

self-control; and to self-control, perseverance; and to perseverance, godliness; and to godliness, mutual affection; and to mutual affection, love. For if you possess these qualities in increasing measure, they will keep you from being ineffective and unproductive in your knowledge of our Lord Jesus Christ.

Listen to the voice of My Spirit within. I will teach you everything you need to know to live a godly life. It's up to you to practice what I teach you. Stay true to the quality of the character modeled for you in My Son, Jesus Christ. *I predestined you to be conformed to the image of My Son* and reflect My glory in ever-increasing measure.

This is how you know that you live in Him and He in you: He has given you of His Spirit. Remain in Me, as I also remain in you. Talk to Me, listen to Me, obey Me, read My Word, pay attention to My Spirit within, and walk in the Spirit rather than the flesh. Grow in your knowledge of Me, and allow the Spirit to transform you into My likeness. All these things contribute to your spiritual growth. *Remain in Me, and the Spirit will produce His fruit in your character. I am the Vine; you are the branches. If you remain in Me and I in you, you will bear much fruit; apart from Me you can do nothing.* Your spiritual growth is achieved by remaining in relationship with My Spirit. Grow in the grace and knowledge of Jesus Christ and His Spirit, and you grow in Me at the same time. It pleases Me very much.

Philippians 4:13; 2 Peter 3:18; 2 Peter 1:5-8;
Romans 8:29; 1 John 4:13; John 15:4-5

Supporting Scripture:

I can do all this through Him Who gives me strength.—Philippians 4:13

But grow in the grace and knowledge of our Lord and Savior Jesus Christ. To Him be glory both now and forever! Amen.—2 Peter 3:18

[5]For this very reason, make every effort to add to your faith goodness; and to goodness, knowledge; [6]and to knowledge, self-control; and to self-control, perseverance; and to perseverance, godliness; [7]and to godliness, mutual affection; and to mutual affection, love. [8]For if you possess these qualities in increasing measure, they will keep you from being ineffective and unproductive in your knowledge of our Lord Jesus Christ.—2 Peter 1:5-8

For those God foreknew He also predestined to be conformed to the image of His Son, that He might be the firstborn among many brothers and sisters.—Romans 8:29

This is how we know that we live in Him and He in us: He has given us of His Spirit.—1 John 4:13

[4]"Remain in Me, as I also remain in you. No branch can bear fruit by itself; it must remain in the vine. Neither can you bear fruit unless you remain in Me. [5]I am the vine; you are the branches. If you remain in Me and I in you, you will bear much fruit; apart from Me you can do nothing."—John 15:4-5

Prayer:

Almighty God, full of grace and mercy, pour out Your love on me today. Allow me to hear the voice of Your Spirit within me and see glimpses of Your heart for me. Father, show me the stagnant areas in my faith, and help me grow in the grace and knowledge of You. You are my King and the Object of my affection. I submit my heart and my will to You and ask that Your Spirit transform me into the likeness of Your Son, Jesus Christ. Lord, let my life be a fragrant offering daily unto You. Holy Spirit, speak to me now as we meet in conversation. In Jesus' name I pray. Amen.

Personal Reflections:

1) From the **Listen to God** section above, pick out a phrase or two that spoke directly to your heart today. Write the words here:

2) As you re-read and think about the words you wrote above, record any additional words or thoughts that come to your mind:

3) Which of the words or thoughts you recorded above might be from God? Underline or highlight them. Does any Scripture come to mind as you re-read what you've written above? If so, write the portion of Scripture that you recall:

4) Turn to the concordance of your Bible and look up one of the words you recalled from Scripture. Scan the verses cited under the word you have referenced in the concordance and record the references of one or two of the verses that the Holy Spirit illumines with special meaning for you today:

5) Turn to each of the references you recorded above. Read the verse and the surrounding passages. Do any additional words or phrases have special meaning for you today? Perhaps something you needed to hear? Wisdom for a problem you face? An answer to a question? A timely word for a difficult circumstance you currently navigate? If so, record the Scripture or words here:

6) What further question(s) do you have for God today? Write them here:

7) Seek God for answers to the question(s) you wrote above. Ask God one of the questions, and then, sit quietly and wait

for His reply. Record the first thought that enters your mind. Write all the thoughts you have as you sit and listen to the Lord:

8) Chances are good that the thoughts you recorded as you sat quietly waiting for the Lord's response were indeed thoughts whispered to you by the Holy Spirit within you. Re-read the thoughts above and ask God to confirm the thoughts that are from Him. Record any new inspirations you hear in your thoughts now:

Identify the Voice:

Re-read the responses you've written to the previous few questions. Run them through the tests below. In each test, the characteristic of God's voice is listed before the OR and the characteristic of Satan's voice is listed after it. Do those thoughts recorded in the section above:

    a. Align with the character of God OR the ways of Satan?
    b. Agree with the Word of God OR contradict it?
    c. Produce the peace of God in your soul OR stir up strife?
    d. Convict you OR condemn you?
    e. Bring spiritual clarity OR confusion?

f. Offer the Lord's wisdom, instruction, comfort, and encouragement OR cause you to feel doubt, fear, worry, or shame?
g. Bring emotional healing OR cause additional emotional pain?

Using the above tests as your guide, draw a line through any thoughts in the previous section that might be from your enemy, the devil. Take a minute to rebuke Satan aloud. Do not believe his lies or buy in to his accusations or condemnations that you identify in your thoughts.

Going Deeper in Two-way Conversation with God:

1) Father, in what areas has my faith lacked growth? (Record what you hear.)

2) Jesus, my Friend, what areas of my character does the Spirit need to transform to make me more like You? (Write down all the thoughts He gives you.)

3) Holy Spirit, how do You transform me? How do You make me more like Jesus? (Journal all the ideas He gives you.)

Review the thoughts God gave you above. Is there a common theme in the impressions you recorded? Perhaps you heard a word that especially warms your heart today? What Scripture comes to mind as you review your notes? Use the concordance of your Bible to look up a word that especially stood out to you or a word that you heard more than once in your thoughts. Scan the list of occurrences of that word cited in Scripture. When you see a verse in the concordance that has special meaning for you today, the Holy Spirit is highlighting that verse for you. Turn to that passage of Scripture and read it. Write the verse here. Then, write all further insights and confirmations the Holy Spirit gives you as you read and ponder God's Word for you today.

Prayer:

Father God, I never want to remain stagnant in my faith. Help me to grow in the image of Christ through the transforming power of Your Spirit. I understand that challenges and trials may produce the most concentrated growth in my spirit. I submit myself to Your leading to transform me however You see fit. I trust that You walk with me in all circumstances and teach me Your ways. Lord, refine me and make me like gold, pure gold (see Zechariah 13:9). In the name of Jesus Christ I pray. Amen.

**BEGINNING OF SIX BONUS DAYS **

Pursuing the Heart of God - Book 2

Day 31 ♥♥ Neither Hot Nor Cold

Ask God:

Dear Father, why do I feel on fire for You sometimes, but many other times, I feel almost nothing, in fact, I feel cold-hearted? My fervor for You is like a tide that ebbs and flows. Father, I know that You are not happy with lukewarm devotion. Lord, I don't want my faith to diminish. I want to be passionate for You at all times. How do I keep that fire burning for You? How do I burn hotter and hotter for You?

Listen to God - A Message from His Heart:

My blessed child, you know My Word that says, *I wish you were either one or the other! So, because you are lukewarm—neither hot nor cold—I am about to spit you out of My mouth.* You know that lukewarm food and drinks of any type are not as pleasing to the palate as either hot or cold ones. So it is with spiritual enthusiasm for Me. I prefer to see you enjoy a burning passion and eagerness for Me in your service and worship. I don't want to force you into anything; it is My hope that you want to spend time with Me in close relationship.

Those whom I love, I rebuke and discipline. So be earnest and repent. Here I am! I stand at the door and knock. If anyone hears My voice and opens the door, I will come in and eat with that person, and they with Me. I discipline you because I love you. I am always waiting at the door of your heart. Will you let Me in? When you do, we will enjoy a sweet communion and companionship.

When you allow other things to take first place in your life, ahead of Me, you are at risk of your fire dying out. Anything that you invest more time in than Me becomes an idol, whether you realize it or not. It doesn't have to be a statue or a physical image that you hold dearly. It can be anything that you adore and revere more than your relationship with Me. *Do not make for yourself an idol in the form of anything I have forbidden. I am a consuming fire, a jealous God.* I am jealous for your love and devotion. I am jealous for your time and relationship.

To keep an engine running smoothly, you must oil it. To keep a lamp burning brightly, you must supply it with oil. Time spent with Me is the oil that will keep your lamp from going out and the lubricant that will keep your engine running. A synthetic oil may promise you longer life, but it is not the real, genuine, life-giving source of fuel for your fire. Only when you spend time with Me will you receive the passion for the things that really matter to Me. Be wise, and do not run out of oil for your lamp. *Keep your lamp burning* brightly and your engine running smoothly with oil of gladness and blessing received only in relationship with Me.

When you are in tune with My Spirit and My heart, your passions will align with Mine. I ignite the fire within you and supply you with the oil to keep it burning. *Remain in Me as I remain in you.* Remain in daily relationship and conversation with Me, and the oil of passion will continue to fuel your internal fire for Me. *I am a consuming Fire. I am jealous* for you because I love you so much. Remain in relationship with Me, and I will ignite a fire within you.

Revelation 3:15-16, 19-20; Deuteronomy 4:23-24;
John 15:4; Psalm 18:28

Supporting Scripture:

[15]"I know your deeds, that you are neither cold nor hot. I wish you were either one or the other! [16]So, because you are lukewarm—neither hot nor cold—I am about to spit you out of My mouth... [19]Those whom I love I rebuke and discipline. So be earnest and repent. [20]Here I am! I stand at the door and knock. If anyone hears My voice and opens the door, I will come in and eat with that person, and they with Me."—Revelation 3:15-16, 19-20

[23]Be careful not to forget the covenant of the LORD your God that He made with you; do not make for yourselves an idol in the form of anything the LORD your God has forbidden. [24]For the LORD your God is a consuming fire, a jealous God.—Deuteronomy 4:23-24

"Remain in Me, as I also remain in you. No branch can bear fruit by itself; it must remain in the vine. Neither can you bear fruit unless you remain in Me."—John 15:4

You, LORD, keep my lamp burning; my God turns my darkness into light.—Psalm 18:28

Prayer:

Dear Father in heaven, thank You for Your consuming fire and jealousy for me. Would it be that I return that fire for You. Let me be jealous for time with You, as You are jealous for time with me. Lord, I am here with You right now, putting You first and desiring to know Your heart and will for my life. Set me ablaze with passion for You. In Jesus' name I pray. Amen.

Personal Reflections:

1) From the **Listen to God** section above, pick out a phrase or two that spoke directly to your heart today. Write the words here:

2) As you re-read and think about the words you wrote above, record any additional words or thoughts that come to your mind:

3) Which of the words or thoughts you recorded above might be from God? Underline or highlight them. Does any Scripture come to mind as you re-read what you've written above? If so, write the portion of Scripture that you recall:

4) Turn to the concordance of your Bible and look up one of the words you recalled from Scripture. Scan the verses cited under the word you have referenced in the concordance and record the references of one or two of the verses that the Holy Spirit illumines with special meaning for you today:

5) Turn to each of the references you recorded above. Read the verse and the surrounding passages. Do any additional words or phrases have special meaning for you today? Perhaps something you needed to hear? Wisdom for a problem you face? An answer to a question? A timely word for a difficult circumstance you currently navigate? If so, record the Scripture or words here:

6) What further question(s) do you have for God today? Write them here:

7) Seek God for answers to the question(s) you wrote above. Ask God one of the questions, and then, sit quietly and wait for His reply. Record the first thought that enters your mind. Write all the thoughts you have as you sit and listen to the Lord:

8) Chances are good that the thoughts you recorded as you sat quietly waiting for the Lord's response were indeed thoughts whispered to you by the Holy Spirit within you. Re-read the thoughts above and ask God to confirm the thoughts that are from Him. Record any new inspirations you hear in your thoughts now:

Identify the Voice:

Re-read the responses you've written to the previous few questions. Run them through the tests below. In each test, the characteristic of God's voice is listed before the OR and the characteristic of Satan's voice is listed after it. Do those thoughts recorded in the section above:

    a. Align with the character of God OR the ways of Satan?
    b. Agree with the Word of God OR contradict it?
    c. Produce the peace of God in your soul OR stir up strife?
    d. Convict you OR condemn you?
    e. Bring spiritual clarity OR confusion?
    f. Offer the Lord's wisdom, instruction, comfort, and encouragement OR cause you to feel doubt, fear, worry, or shame?
    g. Bring emotional healing OR cause additional emotional pain?

Using the above tests as your guide, draw a line through any thoughts in the previous section that might be from your enemy, the devil. Take a minute to rebuke Satan aloud. Do not believe his lies or buy in to his accusations or condemnations that you identify in your thoughts.

Going Deeper in Two-way Conversation with God:

1) Heavenly Father, how do I show You my passion for You? How does that fire for You get ignited in me? (Record every word and thought He gives you.)

2) Jesus, You are the Light of the world. How do I burn brightly for You? Please help me tap into the oil of gladness and blessing that will keep my light burning brightly for You. (Write down all the thoughts He impresses on you.)

3) Holy Spirit, equip me and empower me to put God first in my life. You are the Lover of my soul and my Life-giver. Expand my time, and give me the desire to spend time in relationship with You. What is Your plan for this? (Journal all the words, thoughts, and impressions He gives you right now.)

Review the thoughts God gave you above. Is there a common theme in the impressions you recorded? Perhaps you heard a word that especially warms your heart today? What Scripture comes to mind as you review your notes? Use the concordance of your Bible to look up a word that especially stood out to you or a word that you heard more than once in your thoughts. Scan the list of occurrences of that word cited in Scripture. When you see a verse in the concordance that has special meaning for you today, the Holy Spirit is highlighting that verse for you. Turn to that passage of Scripture and read it. Write the verse here. Then, write all further insights and confirmations the Holy Spirit gives you as you read and ponder God's Word for you today.

Prayer:

Father God, I don't want to be a lukewarm Christ-follower. Lord, ignite in me the fire of passion for You. Pour into me the oil that keeps my lamp burning brightly for You. Lord, keep my lamp burning, and turn my darkness into light (see Psalm 18:28). Please stoke the fire in me and strengthen the flame as I seek a more intimate relationship with You. Lord, give me the desire to remain in You and commit my time to You first. Let me be a well-oiled engine running smoothly in passion and service for You. In Jesus' name I pray. Amen.

Pursuing the Heart of God - Book 2

Day 32 ♥♥ Blessed Are the Merciful

Ask God:

Lord, teach me what it means to be merciful. It is a great gift directly from Your hand. You are a kind, compassionate, and loving Father. You show Your mercy to all Your people through the ages. Help me to be a representation of Your mercy.

Listen to God - A Message from His Heart:

My blessed child, you are created in My likeness. I am *merciful and forgiving*, compassionate and loving, kind and understanding. Practice My ways by the power of My Spirit within you. Show kindness and tenderness to everyone. Be willing to *forgive as you yourself have been forgiven.* Each morning I offer new mercies. Arise each day with a new acceptance of the one you find difficult to love.

I desire genuine devotion, not lip service. Practice My instructions; carry out My commands. Treat others as you want to be treated, with mercy and respect. This may require a change in the way you live. Stop and think before you act or react. Trade in a criticism for a word of kindness. Rather than exercising anger, willingly extend forgiveness. Control your tongue; it can be a double-edged sword—it can build up or tear down—*it can both praise Me or curse humans made in My likeness.* Speak with words of kindness and encouragement, and bring peace to a weary soul.

Be merciful, and you will be shown mercy. Sow seeds of kindness, and you will reap a harvest of kindness. Practice humility with love. Do not wait to be served, but *serve one another humbly in love.* Be compassionate to the hurting, helpful to those in need, and generous with your giving. Exercise grace and mercy whenever you have an opportunity. *Act justly, love mercy, and walk humbly with Me.*

Religious activities mean nothing without personal surrender to the Lord. *The mouth speaks what the heart is full of.* Get your heart right, and be full of blessing and understanding. *For I desire mercy, not sacrifice, and acknowledgment of Me rather than burnt offerings. Be merciful, just as I am merciful.*

In My great mercy, I have given you new birth into a living hope through the resurrection of Jesus Christ from the dead, and into an inheritance that can never perish, spoil or fade. You have new life in Christ and are co-heirs with Him. Experience all the blessing this inheritance provides, both in this life and in life everlasting. As I bless you in this life, be a blessing to others. I have *blessed you to be a blessing.* Bless others with the same attitude of mercy, love, and forgiveness that you have received from Me. *Show mercy and compassion to one another.* I am *rich in mercy,* and you are My heir; therefore, share the wealth of your inheritance in Me.

Daniel 9:9; Colossians 3:13;James 3:9-10; Matthew 5:7;
Galatians 5:13;Micah 6:8; Matthew 12:34;
Hosea 6:6; Luke 6:36; 1 Peter 1:3-5;
Genesis 12:2-3; Zechariah 7:9; Ephesians 2:4-5

Supporting Scripture:

The Lord our God is merciful and forgiving, even though we have rebelled against Him.—Daniel 9:9

Bear with each other and forgive one another if any of you has a grievance against someone. Forgive as the Lord forgave you.—Colossians 3:13

[9]With the tongue we praise our Lord and Father, and with it we curse human beings, who have been made in God's likeness. [10]Out of the same mouth come praise and cursing. My brothers and sisters, this should not be.—James 3:9-10

"Blessed are the merciful, for they will be shown mercy."—Matthew 5:7

You, my brothers and sisters, were called to be free. But do not use your freedom to indulge the flesh; rather, serve one another humbly in love.—Galatians 5:13

He has shown you, O mortal, what is good. And what does the LORD require of you? To act justly and to love mercy and to walk humbly with your God.—Micah 6:8

"...For the mouth speaks what the heart is full of."—Matthew 12:34

"For I desire mercy, not sacrifice, and acknowledgment of God rather than burnt offerings."—Hosea 6:6

"Be merciful, just as your Father is merciful."—Luke 6:36

[3]Praise be to the God and Father of our Lord Jesus Christ! In His great mercy He has given us new birth into a living hope through the resurrection of Jesus Christ from the dead, [4]and into an inheritance that can never perish, spoil or fade. This inheritance is kept in heaven for you, [5]who through faith are shielded by God's power until the coming of the salvation that is ready to be revealed in the last time.—1 Peter 1:3-5

[2]"I will make you into a great nation, and I will bless you; I will make your name great, and you will be a blessing. [3]I will bless those who bless you, and whoever curses you I will curse; and all peoples on earth will be blessed through you."—Genesis 12:2-3

This is what the LORD Almighty said: 'Administer true justice; show mercy and compassion to one another. Do not oppress the widow or the fatherless, the foreigner or the poor. Do not plot evil against each other.'—Zechariah 7:9

⁴But because of His great love for us, God, Who is rich in mercy, ⁵made us alive with Christ even when we were dead in transgressions—it is by grace you have been saved.—Ephesians 2:4-5

Prayer:

Merciful Father in heaven, thank You for Your compassion and grace. You have been so faithful with Your promises and provision. Thank You for Your compassions; they are new every morning (see Lamentations 3:23). Thank You for Your forgiveness and Your peace. Help me to know the meaning of mercy and to pass that gift along to the undeserving one. Holy Spirit of God, share Your heart with me now as we speak one on one. In Jesus' name I pray. Amen.

Personal Reflections:

1) From the **Listen to God** section above, pick out a phrase or two that spoke directly to your heart today. Write the words here:

2) As you re-read and think about the words you wrote above, record any additional words or thoughts that come to your mind:

3) Which of the words or thoughts you recorded above might be from God? Underline or highlight them. Does any Scripture come to mind as you re-read what you've written above? If so, write the portion of Scripture that you recall:

4) Turn to the concordance of your Bible and look up one of the words you recalled from Scripture. Scan the verses cited under the word you have referenced in the concordance and record the references of one or two of the verses that the Holy Spirit illumines with special meaning for you today:

5) Turn to each of the references you recorded above. Read the verse and the surrounding passages. Do any additional words or phrases have special meaning for you today? Perhaps something you needed to hear? Wisdom for a problem you face? An answer to a question? A timely word for a difficult circumstance you currently navigate? If so, record the Scripture or words here:

6) What further question(s) do you have for God today? Write them here:

7) Seek God for answers to the question(s) you wrote above. Ask God one of the questions, and then, sit quietly and wait for His reply. Record the first thought that enters your mind. Write all the thoughts you have as you sit and listen to the Lord:

8) Chances are good that the thoughts you recorded as you sat quietly waiting for the Lord's response were indeed thoughts whispered to you by the Holy Spirit within you. Re-read the thoughts above and ask God to confirm the thoughts that are from Him. Record any new inspirations you hear in your thoughts now:

Identify the Voice:

Re-read the responses you've written to the previous few questions. Run them through the tests below. In each test, the characteristic of God's voice is listed before the OR and the characteristic of Satan's voice is listed after it. Do those thoughts recorded in the section above:

    a. Align with the character of God OR the ways of Satan?
    b. Agree with the Word of God OR contradict it?
    c. Produce the peace of God in your soul OR stir up strife?
    d. Convict you OR condemn you?
    e. Bring spiritual clarity OR confusion?
    f. Offer the Lord's wisdom, instruction, comfort, and encouragement OR cause you to feel doubt, fear, worry, or shame?
    g. Bring emotional healing OR cause additional emotional pain?

Using the above tests as your guide, draw a line through any thoughts in the previous section that might be from your enemy, the devil. Take a minute to rebuke Satan aloud. Do not believe his lies or buy in to his accusations or condemnations that you identify in your thoughts.

Going Deeper in Two-way Conversation with God:

    1) Father God, please remind me of specific ways that You have shown Your mercy to me. (Jot down all the thoughts He gives you.)

2) Lord Jesus, show me ways I might be merciful to others, even specific circumstances recently when I could have shown more mercy. (Write down all the ideas He puts in your heart.)

3) Holy Spirit, empower me with God's character trait of mercy. Fill my heart with mercy specifically for the one who needs to see it from me. Spirit, bring that person to my mind right now, and give me the opportunity to exercise Your loving mercy to this person. (Record what you hear and any examples you are given.)

Review the thoughts God gave you above. Is there a common theme in the impressions you recorded? Perhaps you heard a word that especially warms your heart today? What Scripture comes to mind as you review your notes? Use the concordance of your Bible to look up a word that especially stood out to you or a word that you heard more than once in your thoughts. Scan the list of occurrences of that word cited in Scripture. When you see a verse in the concordance that has special meaning for you today, the Holy Spirit is highlighting that verse for you. Turn to that passage of Scripture and read it. Write the verse here. Then, write all further insights and confirmations the Holy Spirit gives you as you read and ponder God's Word for you today.

Prayer:

Almighty God, You made me in Your image. You are a compassionate, merciful Father. Lord, let me be as kind and forgiving as You are, so that I might be a good representation of Your character. Lord, teach me Your ways, and help me to be merciful that I might be shown Your mercy. Help me be slow to anger and quick to forgive. Give me a heart full of mercy, even when I am not shown any. I desire to live in a manner which is pleasing to You. I humbly give myself to You in order to serve You wholeheartedly. Holy Spirit, teach me Your ways, and empower me to live them out. In Jesus' name I pray. Amen.

Pursuing the Heart of God - Book 2

Day 33 ♥♥ Your Body, My Temple

Ask God:

Oh, Lord, I am in awe that You, the sovereign Ruler of the universe, would choose to make my heart Your dwelling place. I am so blessed and yet so convicted that I should live a life more pleasing to You. However, I still fall short so many times. I don't remember often enough that You live in Me, or I choose to live according to the flesh rather than the Spirit. Please show me Your heart.

Listen to God - A Message from His Heart:

You are My children. I have adopted you as My sons and daughters. You are a member of My family. You have received My life in you. *I have given you My Spirit. I sent My Son to be the Savior of the world. If anyone acknowledges that Jesus is My Son, I live in them and they in Me. So you know and rely on the love I have for you. I am Love. Whoever lives in love lives in Me, and I in them.* I live in you.

Be very careful how you live—not as unwise but as wise. Do not become drunk on wine, but be filled with the Spirit. You are filled with My Spirit and His power—He empowers you to act in a way that attracts non-believers to Me. Draw on that power at all times. *Flee sexual immorality. Do you not know that your bodies are temples of the Holy Spirit, Who is in you, Whom you have received from Me? You are not your own; you were bought at a price. Therefore honor Me with your bodies.* Let the world see and recognize that you do not belong in the world; you belong to Me.

The one who keeps My commands lives in Me, and I in them. And this is how you know that I live in you: You know it by the Spirit I gave you. Now that you know it; go and show it to others. Let them see Me in you. *And if the Spirit of Jesus is living in you, He will also give life to you because of His Spirit Who lives in you,* not only life, but abundant life. *I anointed you, set My seal of ownership on you, and put My Spirit in your hearts as a deposit, guaranteeing what is to come.* You are Mine, and you will spend eternity in heaven with Me. Live your life in confidence with the blessing that life in the Spirit brings now and in the life to come.

You know My promise that *anyone who loves Me will obey My teaching. We will love them, come to them, and make Our home with them.* I am with you always; live with that in mind. Do not defile your body, My home. Keep your heart pure. *Die to sins, and live for the righteousness* provided by My Son. *Let others be won over to Me without words by your behavior when they see the purity and reverence of your lives.*

Your body is My temple. Worship Me with your body. Treat it with care and respect. Take care of your body, My home. Your heart is My sanctuary. Live dedicated to Me, set apart for a higher purpose. *You are My handiwork, created in Christ Jesus to do good works, which I prepared in advance for you to do.* Honor Me in all you do and say. You are Mine; live as such.

1 John 4:13-16; Ephesians 5:15, 18; 1 Corinthians 6:18-20;
1 John 3:24; Romans 8:11; 2 Corinthians 1:21-22; John 14:23;
1 Peter 2:24; 1 Peter 3:1-2; 1 Corinthians 3:16; Ephesians 2:10

Supporting Scripture:

[13]This is how we know that we live in Him and He in us: He has given us of His Spirit. [14]And we have seen and testify that the Father has sent His Son to be the Savior of the world. [15]If anyone acknowledges that Jesus is the Son of God, God lives in them and

they in God. [16]And so we know and rely on the love God has for us. God is love. Whoever lives in love lives in God, and God in them.—1 John 4:13-16

[15]Be very careful, then, how you live—not as unwise but as wise, …[18]Do not get drunk on wine, which leads to debauchery. Instead, be filled with the Spirit,—Ephesians 5:15, 18

[18]Flee from sexual immorality. All other sins a person commits are outside the body, but whoever sins sexually, sins against their own body. [19]Do you not know that your bodies are temples of the Holy Spirit, Who is in you, Whom you have received from God? [20]You are not your own; you were bought at a price. Therefore honor God with your bodies.—1 Corinthians 6:18-20

The one who keeps God's commands lives in Him, and He in them. And this is how we know that He lives in us: We know it by the Spirit He gave us.—1 John 3:24

And if the Spirit of Him Who raised Jesus from the dead is living in you, He Who raised Christ from the dead will also give life to your mortal bodies because of His Spirit Who lives in you.—Romans 8:11

[21]Now it is God Who makes both us and you stand firm in Christ. He anointed us, [22]set His seal of ownership on us, and put His Spirit in our hearts as a deposit, guaranteeing what is to come.—2 Corinthians 1:21-22

Jesus replied, "Anyone who loves Me will obey My teaching. My Father will love them, and We will come to them and make Our home with them."—John 14:23

"He Himself bore our sins" in His body on the cross, so that we might die to sins and live for righteousness; "by His wounds you have been healed."—1 Peter 2:24

[1]Wives, in the same way submit yourselves to your own husbands so that, if any of them do not believe the Word, they may be won over without words by the behavior of their wives, [2]when they see the purity and reverence of your lives.—1 Peter 3:1-2

Don't you know that you yourselves are God's temple and that God's Spirit dwells in your midst?—1 Corinthians 3:16

For we are God's handiwork, created in Christ Jesus to do good works, which God prepared in advance for us to do.—Ephesians 2:10

Prayer:

Heavenly Father, my heart is Your home. You live in me and work through me. Therefore, I can hear the voice of Your Spirit within me as He teaches me more of Your character and Your ways. Holy Spirit of God, speak to me now as we meet in sweet fellowship in Jesus Christ. I am eager to hear a word from You today. Show me more of Your heart through our intimate conversations right now. In Jesus' name I pray. Amen.

Personal Reflections:

1) From the **Listen to God** section above, pick out a phrase or two that spoke directly to your heart today. Write the words here:

2) As you re-read and think about the words you wrote above, record any additional words or thoughts that come to your mind:

3) Which of the words or thoughts you recorded above might be from God? Underline or highlight them. Does any Scripture come to mind as you re-read what you've written above? If so, write the portion of Scripture that you recall:

4) Turn to the concordance of your Bible and look up one of the words you recalled from Scripture. Scan the verses cited under the word you have referenced in the concordance and record the references of one or two of the verses that the Holy Spirit illumines with special meaning for you today:

5) Turn to each of the references you recorded above. Read the verse and the surrounding passages. Do any additional words or phrases have special meaning for you today? Perhaps something you needed to hear? Wisdom for a

problem you face? An answer to a question? A timely word for a difficult circumstance you currently navigate? If so, record the Scripture or words here:

6) What further question(s) do you have for God today? Write them here:

7) Seek God for answers to the question(s) you wrote above. Ask God one of the questions, and then, sit quietly and wait for His reply. Record the first thought that enters your mind. Write all the thoughts you have as you sit and listen to the Lord:

8) Chances are good that the thoughts you recorded as you sat quietly waiting for the Lord's response were indeed thoughts whispered to you by the Holy Spirit within you. Re-read the thoughts above and ask God to confirm the thoughts that are from Him. Record any new inspirations you hear in your thoughts now:

Identify the Voice:

Re-read the responses you've written to the previous few questions. Run them through the tests below. In each test, the characteristic of God's voice is listed before the OR and the characteristic of Satan's voice is listed after it. Do those thoughts recorded in the section above:

  a. Align with the character of God OR the ways of Satan?
  b. Agree with the Word of God OR contradict it?
  c. Produce the peace of God in your soul OR stir up strife?
  d. Convict you OR condemn you?
  e. Bring spiritual clarity OR confusion?
  f. Offer the Lord's wisdom, instruction, comfort, and encouragement OR cause you to feel doubt, fear, worry, or shame?
  g. Bring emotional healing OR cause additional emotional pain?

Using the above tests as your guide, draw a line through any thoughts in the previous section that might be from your enemy, the devil. Take a minute to rebuke Satan aloud. Do not believe his lies or buy in to his accusations or condemnations that you identify in your thoughts.

Going Deeper in Two-way Conversation with God:

  1) Abba Father, please show me any ways that I have offended You with my body. Help me to see the error of my behaviors, and let me repent of my sins. (Record everything He shows you, then confess your sin and turn from these ways.)

2) Jesus, my Savior, teach me what it means to live a life set apart for You. (Write down all thoughts and ideas He gives you.)

3) Holy Spirit, convict me of my sin and help me to live a life of purity and righteousness. Spend some time with me now, cleansing my heart, Your home. (Journal everything you hear from Him.)

Review the thoughts God gave you above. Is there a common theme in the impressions you recorded? Perhaps you heard a word that especially warms your heart today? What Scripture comes to mind as you review your notes? Use the concordance of your Bible to look up a word that especially stood out to you or a word that you heard more than once in your thoughts. Scan the list of occurrences of that word cited in Scripture. When you see a verse in the concordance that has special meaning for you today, the Holy Spirit is highlighting that verse for you. Turn to that passage of Scripture and read it. Write the verse here. Then, write all further insights and confirmations the Holy Spirit gives you as you read and ponder God's Word for you today.

Prayer:

Father in heaven, Whose Spirit lives in me, I want to honor You with my body. I want to live as dead to sin and alive to Christ. Empower me to live a life set apart for You, a life of holiness and purity, free from debauchery. I want to live by Your commands, empowered by Your Spirit to carry out the work You planned for me from the beginning. Thank You for the gift of Your Spirit, Who helps me in my weakness. I yield my spirit to the sanctifying work of Your Holy Spirit in my life. I desire to display the fruit of self-control in my life. Spirit of God, please produce that fruit in me. In the name of Jesus Christ I pray. Amen.

Pursuing the Heart of God - Book 2

Day 34 ♥♥ I Am Your Champion

Ask God:

Lord Jesus, I am most intrigued by the idea of Your being my Champion. It is such a positive, powerful description of Your character. The word Champion itself implies Winner, Victor. You are a Winner! You are the Victor! You were victorious over sin, death, and the grave. You came to earth, taking on the flesh of a man, and yet You remained without sin. Spectacular! Lord, please explain to me Your heart for being my Champion. What does that look like to You? What does that mean for me?

Listen to God - A Message from His Heart:

I am Yahweh, your *warrior* God. I am victorious over all things. I win every battle. I love you and care for you so much that I fight your battles for you, on your behalf. I am with you always. I am your Protector, Defender, Guardian, and Advocate.

I am your Protector. I also give you My protective armor and tools to use in spiritual battles. *Put on My full armor so that when the day of evil comes, you will be strong and stand your ground against the devil's schemes.* I protect you from all evil and the evil one. *Stand firm with the belt of truth buckled around your waist, the breastplate of righteousness in place, and your feet fitted with the readiness that comes from the gospel of peace. Take up the shield of faith, and extinguish the flaming arrows of the evil one. Take the helmet of salvation and the sword of the Spirit, which is the Word of God. Pray in the Spirit on all occasions.*

I am your Defender. I care for you and stand up for you. *I defend the weak and fatherless.* I am the great Shepherd Who cares for His sheep. I defend My sheep against the perils of life. I slay the bear and the wolf. *I lay down My life for the sheep* to keep them safe and free from harm. I laid down My life for you because I love you so deeply.

I am your Guardian. I take care of you. I am concerned about you at all times. I always do what is best for you. *I know the plans I have for you, plans to prosper you and give you hope and a future.* I protect you from the snares of the enemy. I stand watch over you in the night hours, making sure you remain safe. *I neither slumber nor sleep.*

I am your Advocate. I plead your case day and night before My Father in heaven. I live forever, and *I always live to intercede for you.* I am your *great High Priest*, seated at the right hand of God. I am the One Who saves completely. *I am able to empathize with your weakness. I was tempted in every way, yet remained without sin.* My Spirit, Who dwells within you, will empower you with the strength you need to remain without sin.

'Champion' is an all-encompassing word that helps describe the way I feel about you. I love you so much, I want to protect you from all evil. *I will watch over your coming and going both now and forevermore.* I go before you and behind you. I stand at your side in support of you through all your battles and challenges. I *uphold your cause* and plead your case. I am your biggest Cheerleader, and I care about every aspect of your life. I love you completely. I always desire My best for you. Focus on Me! I am on your side! When I am for you, who can be against you?

Exodus 15:3; Ephesians 6:10-18; Psalm 82:3;
John 10:11; Jeremiah 29:11; Psalm 121:3-4;
Hebrews 7:24-25; Hebrews 4:15; Psalm 121:7

Supporting Scripture:

"The LORD is a warrior; the LORD is His name."—Exodus 15:3

The Armor of God [10]Finally, be strong in the Lord and in His mighty power. [11]Put on the full armor of God, so that you can take your stand against the devil's schemes. [12]For our struggle is not against flesh and blood, but against the rulers, against the authorities, against the powers of this dark world and against the spiritual forces of evil in the heavenly realms. [13]Therefore put on the full armor of God, so that when the day of evil comes, you may be able to stand your ground, and after you have done everything, to stand. [14]Stand firm then, with the belt of truth buckled around your waist, with the breastplate of righteousness in place, [15]and with your feet fitted with the readiness that comes from the gospel of peace. [16]In addition to all this, take up the shield of faith, with which you can extinguish all the flaming arrows of the evil one. [17]Take the helmet of salvation and the sword of the Spirit, which is the Word of God. [18]And pray in the Spirit on all occasions with all kinds of prayers and requests. With this in mind, be alert and always keep on praying for all the Lord's people.—Ephesians 6:10-18

Defend the weak and the fatherless; uphold the cause of the poor and the oppressed.—Psalm 82:3

"I am the good shepherd. The good shepherd lays down His life for the sheep."—John 10:11

"For I know the plans I have for you," declares the LORD, "plans to prosper you and not to harm you, plans to give you hope and a future."—Jeremiah 29:11

[3]He will not let your foot slip—He who watches over you will not slumber; [4]indeed, He who watches over Israel will neither slumber nor sleep.—Psalm 121:3-4

[24]But because Jesus lives forever, He has a permanent priesthood. [25]Therefore He is able to save completely those who come to God through Him, because He always lives to intercede for them.—Hebrews 7:24-25

For we do not have a high priest who is unable to empathize with our weaknesses, but we have one Who has been tempted in every way, just as we are—yet He did not sin.—Hebrews 4:15

The LORD will keep you from all harm—He will watch over your life; the LORD will watch over your coming and going both now and forevermore.—Psalm 121:7

Prayer:

Dear God, I am humbled again by the greatness of Your love for me. You care about me when no one else does. You watch over me day and night to protect me from all perils. Lord, thank You for loving me, caring for me, protecting me, defending me, guarding me, and being my Champion. I am so blessed to be Your child, to be so completely loved by You. I scarcely can take it in. Please continue to speak to me now as we spend a few moments together alone. Allow me to clearly hear Your voice and thoughts within me. Eliminate all distractions, and help me focus my heart in the direction of Yours. In Jesus' name I pray. Amen.

Personal Reflections:

1) From the **Listen to God** section above, pick out a phrase or two that spoke directly to your heart today. Write the words here:

2) As you re-read and think about the words you wrote above, record any additional words or thoughts that come to your mind:

3) Which of the words or thoughts you recorded above might be from God? Underline or highlight them. Does any Scripture come to mind as you re-read what you've written above? If so, write the portion of Scripture that you recall:

4) Turn to the concordance of your Bible and look up one of the words you recalled from Scripture. Scan the verses cited under the word you have referenced in the concordance and record the references of one or two of the verses that the Holy Spirit illumines with special meaning for you today:

5) Turn to each of the references you recorded above. Read the verse and the surrounding passages. Do any additional words or phrases have special meaning for you today? Perhaps something you needed to hear? Wisdom for a problem you face? An answer to a question? A timely word for a difficult circumstance you currently navigate? If so, record the Scripture or words here:

6) What further question(s) do you have for God today? Write them here:

7) Seek God for answers to the question(s) you wrote above. Ask God one of the questions, and then, sit quietly and wait for His reply. Record the first thought that enters your mind. Write all the thoughts you have as you sit and listen to the Lord:

8) Chances are good that the thoughts you recorded as you sat quietly waiting for the Lord's response were indeed

thoughts whispered to you by the Holy Spirit within you. Re-read the thoughts above and ask God to confirm the thoughts that are from Him. Record any new inspirations you hear in your thoughts now:

Identify the Voice:

Re-read the responses you've written to the previous few questions. Run them through the tests below. In each test, the characteristic of God's voice is listed before the OR and the characteristic of Satan's voice is listed after it. Do those thoughts recorded in the section above:

a. Align with the character of God OR the ways of Satan?
b. Agree with the Word of God OR contradict it?
c. Produce the peace of God in your soul OR stir up strife?
d. Convict you OR condemn you?
e. Bring spiritual clarity OR confusion?
f. Offer the Lord's wisdom, instruction, comfort, and encouragement OR cause you to feel doubt, fear, worry, or shame?
g. Bring emotional healing OR cause additional emotional pain?

Using the above tests as your guide, draw a line through any thoughts in the previous section that might be from your enemy, the devil. Take a minute to rebuke Satan aloud. Do not believe his lies or buy in to his accusations or condemnations that you identify in your thoughts.

Going Deeper in Two-way Conversation with God:

1) Warrior God, help me understand how You fight for me daily. (Record the thoughts He gives you.)

2) Jesus, my good Shepherd, please describe to me how You take care of me as Your sheep. (Write all words and ideas given to you right now.)

3) Holy Spirit, my Advocate, intercede for me, and give me access to God's heart for me with regard to a current battle I face. (Record all thoughts and impressions you receive.)

Review the thoughts God gave you above. Is there a common theme in the impressions you recorded? Perhaps you heard a word that especially warms your heart today? What Scripture comes to mind as you review your notes? Use the concordance of your Bible to look up a word that especially stood out to you or a word that you heard more than once in your thoughts. Scan the list of occurrences of that word cited in Scripture. When you see a verse in the concordance that has special meaning for you today, the Holy Spirit is highlighting that verse for you. Turn to that passage of Scripture and read it. Write the verse here. Then, write all further insights and confirmations the Holy Spirit gives you as you read and ponder God's Word for you today.

Prayer:

Father, Son, and Holy Spirit, thank You for meeting with me to share more of Your heart with me and for me. I am so grateful for Your omniscience, omnipotence, and omnipresence in my life. You know all, control all, and inhabit all. I am so blessed to have You, the Almighty Warrior God, on my side, in my corner. Thank You for Your protection, defense, and intercession. I am eternally grateful that You care for me so completely and thoroughly, meeting all my needs and desires, *in all things working for my good* (see Romans 8:28). In Jesus' name I pray. Amen.

Day 35 ♥♥ Rescuer and Redeemer

Ask God:

Lord, I have firsthand knowledge of You as my Rescuer and Redeemer. You rescued me from a life of sin and mediocrity. You redeemed me with Your own life to free me from the bondage of sin. You delivered me from the captivity of my enemy's lies and *redeemed my life from the pit* of depression (see Psalm 103:4). You set my feet on solid ground and began the rebuilding process in me. You exchanged the lies I believed for Your perfect truth and built up my faith and confidence in You. You prepared me to fulfill the purpose You created me for and gave me a new reason to live. Thank You for loving me enough to rescue me and redeem me from the life I created for myself. "May these words of my mouth and this meditation of my heart be pleasing in your sight, LORD, my Rock and my Redeemer."—Psalm 19:14

Listen to God - A Message from His Heart:

My beloved child, I am so excited that you recognize, appreciate, and bear witness to My transforming work in your life. I pulled you up *out of the mud and mire.* I set your feet on solid ground—My *firm* foundation—and I began the rebuilding process in you. You have gone to difficult places, brokenness in your heart, and allowed Me to heal you with My truth. *The Son has set you free, so you are free indeed.*

You have put Me first in your life by remaining in close relationship with Me. You meet with Me, pray to Me, listen to Me, and obey Me. I cherish you, and I treasure the time we spend together in the Spirit. As a child who runs home from school and throws open the door to tell his family about his day, I can't wait for you to run through the door to our secret meeting place, where I can hold you in My arms and encourage you with My love and support.

On those days when you have been bullied and underappreciated, I love to uphold you and support you through your challenges. When you are knocked down, I pick you back up and strengthen your spirit. When your soul has been depleted, My Spirit refreshes yours. I give you spiritual nourishment with My bread from heaven. I feed your soul and satisfy your thirst. I am your All in All. I am Everything you need.

I rescue you from the mundane and give you meaning and purpose for your life, doing the work I have *prepared in advance for you to do*. I redeemed your life of sin and rebellion and exchanged it for a life of holiness and righteousness, for the glory of My Name's sake. *I rescued you because I delighted in you.* You are My beloved child. All that I have belongs to you. I am a loving Father Who desires a deeper intimacy with you. I created you to love you, and I saved you so that you could love Me and relate to Me. Let's get together again soon, My friend. I have so much more of My heart to share with you.

Psalm 103:4; Psalm 40:2;
John 8:36; Ephesians 2:10; Psalm 18:19

Supporting Scripture:

Who redeems your life from the pit and crowns you with love and compassion—Psalm 103:4

He lifted me out of the slimy pit, out of the mud and mire; He set my feet on a rock and gave me a firm place to stand.—Psalm 40:2

"So if the Son sets you free, you will be free indeed."—John 8:36

For we are God's handiwork, created in Christ Jesus to do good works, which God prepared in advance for us to do.—Ephesians 2:10

He brought me out into a spacious place; He rescued me because He delighted in me.—Psalm 18:19

Prayer:

Dear Jesus, I camp on the verse from Psalm 49:15, "But God will redeem me from the realm of the dead; He will surely take me to Himself." Lord, You have so graciously done that for me, and I am forever grateful to You. Thank You for rescuing me from my own dead inner spirit and producing new life in me by the indwelling presence and power of Your Holy Spirit. Please speak to me now and share Your heart with me today. In the power of Jesus' name I pray. Amen.

Personal Reflections:

1) From the **Listen to God** section above, pick out a phrase or two that spoke directly to your heart today. Write the words here:

2) As you re-read and think about the words you wrote above, record any additional words or thoughts that come to your mind:

3) Which of the words or thoughts you recorded above might be from God? Underline or highlight them. Does any Scripture come to mind as you re-read what you've written above? If so, write the portion of Scripture that you recall:

4) Turn to the concordance of your Bible and look up one of the words you recalled from Scripture. Scan the verses cited under the word you have referenced in the concordance and record the references of one or two of the verses that the Holy Spirit illumines with special meaning for you today:

5) Turn to each of the references you recorded above. Read the verse and the surrounding passages. Do any additional words or phrases have special meaning for you today? Perhaps something you needed to hear? Wisdom for a problem you face? An answer to a question? A timely word for a difficult circumstance you currently navigate? If so, record the Scripture or words here:

6) What further question(s) do you have for God today? Write them here:

7) Seek God for answers to the question(s) you wrote above. Ask God one of the questions, and then, sit quietly and wait for His reply. Record the first thought that enters your mind. Write all the thoughts you have as you sit and listen to the Lord:

8) Chances are good that the thoughts you recorded as you sat quietly waiting for the Lord's response were indeed thoughts whispered to you by the Holy Spirit within you. Re-read the thoughts above and ask God to confirm the thoughts that are from Him. Record any new inspirations you hear in your thoughts now:

Identify the Voice:

Re-read the responses you've written to the previous few questions. Run them through the tests below. In each test, the characteristic of God's voice is listed before the OR and the characteristic of Satan's voice is listed after it. Do those thoughts recorded in the section above:

    a. Align with the character of God OR the ways of Satan?
    b. Agree with the Word of God OR contradict it?
    c. Produce the peace of God in your soul OR stir up strife?
    d. Convict you OR condemn you?
    e. Bring spiritual clarity OR confusion?
    f. Offer the Lord's wisdom, instruction, comfort, and encouragement OR cause you to feel doubt, fear, worry, or shame?

g. Bring emotional healing OR cause additional emotional pain?

Using the above tests as your guide, draw a line through any thoughts in the previous section that might be from your enemy, the devil. Take a minute to rebuke Satan aloud. Do not believe his lies or buy in to his accusations or condemnations that you identify in your thoughts.

Going Deeper in Two-way Conversation with God:

1) Father, thank You for reaching down to rescue me from a life that did not glorify You as You deserve. Please share with me Your heart and Your reason for saving me. (Record all the thoughts and ideas He gives you.)

2) Jesus, thank You for paying the price of my redemption. Please share Your heart with me on what You want me to do with this information. (Write all ideas that pop into your head right now.)

3) Holy Spirit, enable me to enjoy a closer walk with You by opening my ears to hear what You share with me now. (Jot down all words and thoughts that come to mind.)

Review the thoughts God gave you above. Is there a common theme in the impressions you recorded? Perhaps you heard a word that especially warms your heart today? What Scripture comes to mind as you review your notes? Use the concordance of your Bible to look up a word that especially stood out to you or a word that you heard more than once in your thoughts. Scan the list of occurrences of that word cited in Scripture. When you see a verse in the concordance that has special meaning for you today, the Holy Spirit is highlighting that verse for you. Turn to that passage of Scripture and read it. Write the verse here. Then, write all further insights and confirmations the Holy Spirit gives you as you read and ponder God's Word for you today.

Prayer:

Heavenly Father, thank You for sharing Your heart and thoughts with me just now through the voice of the Holy Spirit. I appreciate the closeness I feel when we meet. Help me to feel Your presence with me even when I don't hear Your voice in my thoughts. You remind me that You are always with me; *You never leave me nor forsake me* (see Joshua 1:5). You are with me at all times, speaking to me and guiding me in the way I should go. I appreciate the love and affection You poured out on me today. Thank You for sharing Your heart with me. In Jesus' name I pray. Amen.

Pursuing the Heart of God - Book 2

Day 36 ♥♥ Put Me First – Seek Me in the Morning

Ask God:

Lord God Almighty, help me to get up a few minutes early each morning to put You first by meeting with the Holy Spirit alone, one on one, away from all noise and distractions. I know my days end better when they begin with You. You are the First and the Last and everything in between (see Revelation 22:13). You meet all my needs and fulfill all my longings. Lord, thank You for loving me more than I love myself. Please share with me today another piece of Your heart. This morning, Lord, hear my voice; I lay my requests before You and wait expectantly (see Psalm 5:3).

Listen to God - A Message from His Heart:

O My sweet child, do not put off meeting with Me. *Seek Me first* thing in the morning before your feet hit the floor. Acknowledge Me and speak with Me before you get out of bed. Think of Me while you drink your first cup of coffee. Make time to meet with Me, if only for a few moments, before you begin your day. Let's get you started in the right direction. My intentions for you are good.

I do not require too much from you. I simply want to say hello. I will love you and encourage you for the day that waits ahead. I know what you will face each day, and I would love to walk you through your challenges and your triumphs, your sorrows and your joys, your work and your play. I created you so I could love you, and I care deeply about you. I want to be involved in your life. No detail is too small for Me. Please put Me first, and *seek Me with all your heart*, in everything you do. *Those who seek Me find Me.*

I am with you all day, whether you acknowledge Me or not, but I would love to partner with you. *I know the plans I have for you, plans to prosper you and not to harm you, plans to give you hope and a future.* Would you like to check with Me before you run ahead and make your own plans? I know what's best for you, and I would love to see you thrive and succeed.

No matter what, you do not go it alone. I am by your side at all times. I know you enjoy your independence and control, but I would love for you to depend on Me. I will not let you down. Consult Me for your wisdom and answers to your questions. *Call to Me, and I will answer you; I will tell you things you do not know.* Do not be the master at controlling your own life and destiny; I am in control of all things, I know all things, and *in all things I work for your good.*

Worship Me with gladness. I am God. I made you, you are Mine. *Worship Me in Spirit and in truth. Ascribe to Me the glory due My name, and worship Me in the splendor of My holiness. I am the Alpha and the Omega, the First and the Last, the Beginning and the End.* I am all you need. I am sufficient. You can depend on Me for all things. Seek Me first, and everything else will fall into place as it should. I love you, My child, more than you will ever comprehend.

Isaiah 55:6; Matthew 6:33; Proverbs 8:17; Jeremiah 29:11;
Jeremiah 33:3; Romans 8:28; Psalm 100:2;
John 4:24; 1 Chronicles 16:29; Revelation 22:13

Supporting Scripture:

"But seek first His kingdom and His righteousness, and all these things will be given to you as well."—Matthew 6:33

"I love those who love Me, and those who seek Me find Me."—Proverbs 8:17

"For I know the plans I have for you," declares the LORD, "plans to prosper you and not to harm you, plans to give you hope and a future."—Jeremiah 29:11

"Call to Me and I will answer you and tell you great and unsearchable things you do not know."—Jeremiah 33:3

And we know that in all things God works for the good of those who love Him, who have been called according to His purpose.—Romans 8:28

Worship the LORD with gladness; come before Him with joyful songs.—Psalm 100:2

"God is spirit, and His worshipers must worship in the Spirit and in truth."—John 4:24

Ascribe to the LORD the glory due His name; bring an offering and come before Him. Worship the LORD in the splendor of His holiness.—1 Chronicles 16:29

"I am the Alpha and the Omega, the First and the Last, the Beginning and the End."—Revelation 22:13

Prayer:

Father God, thank You for loving me so completely. Help me to partner with the Holy Spirit as He guides me through my entire day. Holy Spirit, jog my memory to think of You all day long. Allow me to hear all the whispers You speak throughout the day. Help me remember to seek You first in all I do. When I do, I will find You, and You will show me what's best for me. Holy Spirit, I am seeking You right now for Your counsel and Your wisdom for my day. Please show me what You want me to see, hear, and know. In Jesus' name I pray. Amen.

Personal Reflections:

1) From the **Listen to God** section above, pick out a phrase or two that spoke directly to your heart today. Write the words here:

2) As you re-read and think about the words you wrote above, record any additional words or thoughts that come to your mind:

3) Which of the words or thoughts you recorded above might be from God? Underline or highlight them. Does any Scripture come to mind as you re-read what you've written above? If so, write the portion of Scripture that you recall:

4) Turn to the concordance of your Bible and look up one of the words you recalled from Scripture. Scan the verses cited under the word you have referenced in the concordance and

record the references of one or two of the verses that the Holy Spirit illumines with special meaning for you today:

5) Turn to each of the references you recorded above. Read the verse and the surrounding passages. Do any additional words or phrases have special meaning for you today? Perhaps something you needed to hear? Wisdom for a problem you face? An answer to a question? A timely word for a difficult circumstance you currently navigate? If so, record the Scripture or words here:

6) What further question(s) do you have for God today? Write them here:

7) Seek God for answers to the question(s) you wrote above. Ask God one of the questions, and then, sit quietly and wait for His reply. Record the first thought that enters your mind. Write all the thoughts you have as you sit and listen to the Lord:

8) Chances are good that the thoughts you recorded as you sat quietly waiting for the Lord's response were indeed thoughts whispered to you by the Holy Spirit within you. Re-read the thoughts above and ask God to confirm the thoughts that are from Him. Record any new inspirations you hear in your thoughts now:

Identify the Voice:

Re-read the responses you've written to the previous few questions. Run them through the tests below. In each test, the characteristic of God's voice is listed before the OR and the characteristic of Satan's voice is listed after it. Do those thoughts recorded in the section above:

a. Align with the character of God OR the ways of Satan?
b. Agree with the Word of God OR contradict it?
c. Produce the peace of God in your soul OR stir up strife?
d. Convict you OR condemn you?
e. Bring spiritual clarity OR confusion?
f. Offer the Lord's wisdom, instruction, comfort, and encouragement OR cause you to feel doubt, fear, worry, or shame?
g. Bring emotional healing OR cause additional emotional pain?

Using the above tests as your guide, draw a line through any thoughts in the previous section that might be from your enemy, the devil. Take a minute to rebuke Satan aloud. Do not believe his lies or buy in to his accusations or condemnations that you identify in your thoughts.

Going Deeper in Two-way Conversation with God:

1) Lord God, I am putting You first today by spending this time with You. Please share Your heart with me now. What is it that You want me to hear and know for today? (Record all thoughts and words that come to mind.)

2) Jesus, You are the ultimate example of putting God first and seeking Him alone in the morning. Please show me how to do that in my busy life. Tell me what will work for me. (Write the ideas and promptings that flow through your thoughts.)

3) Holy Spirit, please nudge me now to walk in partnership with You. Let me see a glimpse of Your work in my life, in my day. What do You want me to hear and know today? (Jot down what He impresses on you right now.)

Review the thoughts God gave you above. Is there a common theme in the impressions you recorded? Perhaps you heard a word that especially warms your heart today? What Scripture comes to mind as you review your notes? Use the concordance of your Bible to look up a word that especially stood out to you or a word that you heard more than once in your thoughts. Scan the list of occurrences of that word cited in Scripture. When you see a verse in the concordance that has special meaning for you today, the Holy Spirit is highlighting that verse for you. Turn to that passage of Scripture and read it. Write the verse here. Then, write all further insights and confirmations the Holy Spirit gives you as you read and ponder God's Word for you today.

Prayer:

Heavenly Father, thank You for meeting with me today to show me the importance of putting You first in my life. You have all things under Your control. I need not fret, worry, or strive to create my own destiny because You have marked out a path for me. You have my best interests at heart, and You will see that I prosper in all I do, in all You have planned for me. Help me fulfill the purpose for which You created me. In Jesus' precious name I pray. Amen

Conclusion

It is my prayer that over the last couple months, these two books have enabled you to establish or re-establish an intimate relationship with the King of kings and Lord of lords. In these two 30-day journeys to deeper intimacy with God, you put Him first, making time to meet alone with God, away from the crowds and noise, in an effort to pursue His heart and listen to the voice of His Holy Spirit within you.

I hope you're enjoying an increased awareness and understanding of the third Person of the Trinity, the Spirit of Truth, Who lives in your heart and works diligently to teach you, guide you, comfort you, encourage you, empower you, and sanctify you.

I pray that you identified how to discern God's voice from your own thoughts and the voice of your enemy. I encourage you to daily clothe yourself in the armor of God (see Ephesians 6:10-18) and stand firm in the battle against the evil one. I hope you are better equipped to identify the voice of Satan in your thoughts, rebuke him, and claim your victory over the enemy in the name of Jesus Christ, by His shed blood at Calvary.

It is my hope that your spiritual ears are more in tune with the voice of God within you. I pray your listening skills have been sharpened so that you are better able to hear the Lord's whispers in your thoughts, His personal encouragements and instructions specifically for you and your circumstances—His rhēma—while also strengthening your understanding of His logos—God-breathed Scripture.

I am pleased you have allowed me to share with you one way to pursue the heart of God. If using this method successfully increased your connection and communication with the Lord in any aspect, please don't stop here. Continue to meet with Him daily. Use the tools that work best for you personally as you meet with the Lord. Whether it's using a devotional to jump-start your time with God or just sitting quietly with Him, asking Him questions and waiting for His reply—whatever you do, work at it with all your heart (see Colossians 3:23). Seek the Lord while He may be found (see Isaiah 55:6). You will find Him if you seek Him with all your heart and with all your soul (see Deuteronomy 4:29).

In John 8:47, God's Word promises, "Whoever belongs to God hears what God says…" You belong to God; therefore, you *do* hear what He says. Expect and believe—you hear the voice of the Holy Spirit Who dwells in your heart. He is with you always. Seek Him first in all things. Listen and obey.

Blessings in Christ Jesus,

Sindy Nagel

Purchase Sindy's other books on Amazon.com

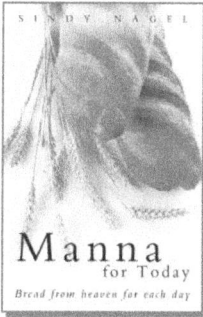

Manna for Today:
Bread from Heaven for Each Day

ISBN: 978-1-4497-6704-4 (Paperback)
ISBN: 978-1-4497-6705-1 (Hardcover)
ISBN: 978-1-4497-6703-7 (Kindle)

Publisher: WestBow Press
(A Division of Thomas Nelson)

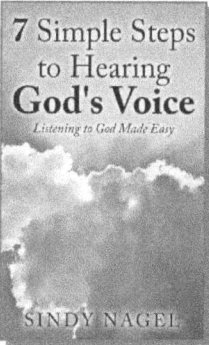

Hearing God's Voice Series (Book 1)

7 Simple Steps to Hearing God's Voice:
Listening to God Made Easy

ISBN: 978-0-9969934-0-1 (Paperback)
ISBN: 978-0-9969934-7-0 (Kindle)
ISBN: 978-0-9969934-3-2 (Audio Book)

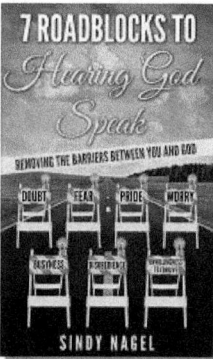

Hearing God's Voice Series (Book 2)

7 Roadblocks to Hearing God Speak:
Removing the Barriers Between You
and God

ISBN: 978-0-9969934-6-3 (Paperback)
ISBN: 978-0-9969934-9-4 (Kindle)
ISBN: 978-0-9969934-2-5 (Audio Book)

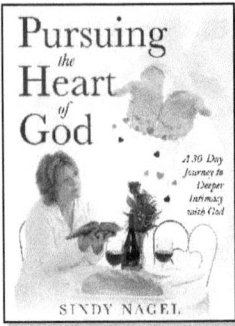

Pursuing the Heart of God Series (Book 1)

Pursuing the Heart of God: A 30-Day Journey to Deeper Intimacy with God

ISBN: 978-0-9969934-1-8 (Paperback)
ISBN: 978-0-9969934-8-7 (Kindle)
ISBN: 978-1-7368521-0-1 (Audio Book)

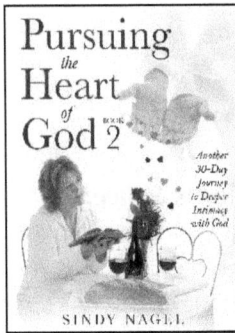

Pursuing the Heart of God Series (Book 2)

Pursuing the Heart of God - Book 2: Another 30-Day Journey to Deeper Intimacy with God

ISBN: 978-0-9969934-4-9 (Paperback)
ISBN: 978-0-9969934-5-6 (Kindle)
ISBN: 978-1-7368521-1-8 (Audio Book)

Follow Sindy's Blog
www.sindynagel.com

Follow Sindy on Facebook
www.facebook.com/SindyNagel.Author/

Author Email
sindynagel612@aol.com

www.ingramcontent.com/pod-product-compliance
Lightning Source LLC
LaVergne TN
LVHW051038080426
835508LV00019B/1578